Acts

Acts
Catching Up with the Spirit

Acts
978-1-5018-9455-8
978-1-5018-9456-5 eBook

Acts DVD
978-1-5018-9459-6

Acts Leader Guide
978-1-5018-9457-2
978-1-5018-9458-9 eBook

MATTHEW L. SKINNER

ACTS

CATCHING UP WITH THE SPIRIT

Abingdon Press / Nashville

Acts

Library of Congress Control Number: 2019957186

978-1-5018-9455-8

20 21 22 23 24 25 26 27 28 29 — 10 9 8 7 6 5 4 3 2 1
MANUFACTURED IN THE UNITED STATES OF AMERICA

With love and gratitude to

Barbara Joyner
and
Betsey Skinner

strong women
each in her own way

Contents

Contents

Preface

If you're interested in learning what the Acts of the Apostles has to say and how it can contribute to your efforts to live faithfully today, this book was written for you. I don't assume that you, the reader, already possess any deep knowledge about Acts, and so this book provides a short and lively introduction to one of the New Testament's longer and more neglected writings. But neither do I assume that you aren't willing to think diligently or creatively about Acts. Whether Acts is already familiar or totally foreign to you, I assume you're willing to take me seriously if I propose that reading it in a particular way—with attention to specific features of the stories it tells—might inspire us to consider anew what Christian faith and life should look like in our complicated age. I'll be grateful if this experience also shifts or enlarges your perspectives on the Bible in general and on its usefulness.

The purpose of this book therefore goes beyond simply understanding Acts better. I want the time you spend with Acts to encourage you along your own path toward knowing God and adopting habits of living generously with our neighbors, whether they consider themselves members of a

Christian congregation or not. From teaching about Acts in numerous settings I've learned that exploring Acts, if we ask the right kinds of questions, has a way of igniting our imaginations. I'm talking about our *theological* imaginations, how we think about God and sort through the big questions that Acts lays on the table: What is God like? How does the good news about Jesus Christ redirect my points of view and priorities? What should God's people ("the church") be doing in response to God's mercy? How do we negotiate the challenges of living faithfully in a complex and changing world? What sort of impact might the good news have beyond the church, as Christians influence their societies?

Acts first offered answers to those questions for believers living more than 1900 years ago. Christians have ruminated over similar subjects throughout the church's history. This book works together with Acts in nourishing your imagination as you consider the questions. I hope it spurs you to think about what it means to catch up with the Holy Spirit as you seek to encounter God in your own circumstances.

Like any biblical book, Acts takes us to a different time and place. The narrative assumes we know something about what the ancient world was like—concerning ancient religious beliefs, economic realities, social expectations, cultural norms, and political tensions. As an introduction to Acts and its enduring value for Christian readers, this book cannot pause to give detailed comments on all of those topics when they arise. A thick study Bible or some of the books I recommend in the "For Further Reading" section will help you find additional answers and dig deeper into individual biblical passages. Right now, the aim is to get you started—or restarted—on a rich journey through the pages of Acts and its story about Jesus' followers as they undertake the exciting and sometimes confusing work of catching up with the Holy Spirit.

Introduction

I enjoy reading the Book of Acts, but sometimes it scares me.

I'm drawn to Acts because it's one of the wildest books in the Bible. It describes events that are so unfamiliar to my life and my own experiences as a person of faith. Miraculous prison escapes, rapidly growing Christian communities, otherwise ordinary people suddenly speaking in languages they have never learned, appearances by angels, rousing speeches and sermons that either convince or infuriate huge crowds, a shipwreck, people sharing all their money with one another for the common good, extraordinary healings, massive public demonstrations, and an unwavering sense of hope—so many aspects of Acts make me feel like I've lived an overly safe and sheltered life. The book is stirring, because it tells a story in which anything seems possible now that a new day has dawned. Acts urges me to dream bigger and expect more.

I'm not frightened of a life of adventure and excitement. Sign me up for that. What scares me is the sense that the story in Acts often seems too easy. Groups of believers agree with one another and their leaders a lot. Some people conveniently escape hardship and physical harm over and over. Faith does not have to grapple with doubt. Villains suffer comeuppances and honored heroes either have no faults or are never called to account for their faults. Acts does not resemble the way the world works, from my point of view. Not only is my life more ordinary; it's also more nuanced and ambiguous. My personal experience of faith in Christ involves much more trial and error, unanswered prayer, cranky congregations, valuable lessons learned from other religious traditions, and even dark nights of the soul. Acts has a way of making some of us worry that we're doing something wrong in how we live as Christians. Or maybe God took an extended hiatus from the world after the story told in Acts ended.

That explains why I have so much fun wrestling with Acts; it makes me think and prompts me to consider the ancient church's experiences as well as my own. Those aren't always typical ways people respond to the Bible, because a lot of us were once conditioned to assume that the Bible's purpose is to answer our "What do I need to know?" questions. But who wants to place their hope in information? Faith is not about committing yourself to learn and believe the One Correct and Unchallengeable List of Doctrines. Faith is much more experiential and personal. It should make us squirm. It might make us push back.

As we explore Acts together, I'm going to ask you not to read Acts like you would read a modern history book, such as one that analyzes the economic and political causes of the Great Depression, drawing on statistics and quotations from speeches preserved in the Congressional Record. Acts is not that kind of a book. Actually, I don't think any book produced around the first century was quite like that. Our modern tendency to consider "fact" and "fiction" as entirely separate categories would have been lost on ancient historians. Some parts of Acts strike me as incredible, but I need to hold my questions and skepticism alongside an appreciation for what Acts is trying to convey.

Acts is a bit of a romp. It's as entertaining and provocative as it is informational. That's what ancient audiences expected from people who wrote histories—not meticulously objective, detached reporting but writing that made you feel like you were there. Accordingly, Acts is interested in molding the perceptions we live with concerning God and the world.

As you read Acts, then, think about the kinds of people and communities it describes. Consider what makes faith and obedience easy for them or difficult for them. How does Acts perceive the world and the difference that the good news about Jesus Christ makes for the world? The thrills and exaggeration that seep from the storytelling awaken my imagination and nudge me to ponder how we encounter and speak about God in the world today. I hope they urge you to put away cautious rationality for a little while and make you wonder about what kinds of things are possible for people of faith and the communities in which we live. What you do with your expanded and expectant imagination—how you let it affect your life and faith—is up to you. Just know that reading Acts has the capacity to change you. For Acts is a book determined to remind you what it means to be a follower of Jesus Christ.

Following Jesus involves much more than imitating a historical figure. Acts implies we still follow Jesus in the world today. Acts insists that Jesus remains present in human experience through the Holy Spirit, urging believers to keep pace so we can rediscover God among us in the midst of whatever will happen next.

Acts 1:1-2

The beginning of a story that already began

Get ready, because in the very first verse of Acts we have to make an important decision that will influence how we read the rest of the story. More specifically, we have to figure out which translators to trust. Before we get to that, let's put the opening two verses into context.

Right away Acts declares it was written by the same person who wrote the Gospel according to Luke. Read Luke 1:1-4 to examine more evidence. Moreover, Luke and Acts share much in common in terms of style, vocabulary, themes, syntax, and general outlook. Acts, therefore, is a sequel to Luke. That's worth noting, because the sheer existence of a sequel means someone thought the story of Jesus and his significance did not end with his resurrection and ascension. There was more to tell.

Back to our translation decision. Everyone agrees that the mention of the "first book" or "former account" in Acts 1:1 refers to the Gospel of Luke. The question for us to consider lies in what the author says in that verse about Luke. Some published Bible translations (such as the NRSV) say that Acts refers to Luke as the book about "all that Jesus did and taught." Other translations (such as the ESV) say that Luke describes "all that Jesus began to do and teach." The first option implies that Jesus has completed his tasks and now the story of the church can commence. The second option implies that Jesus, even though he no longer physically walks the earth, is still doing and teaching. The story of what he "began" to do in Luke continues, now in the experience of the church and the wider world.

If I explain debates over Greek grammar you'll stop reading, so I'll simply say we're choosing the second translation.

I'm convinced it's the correct choice, judging from a strictly grammatical point of view. You'll have to trust me on that. More interesting than the grammar, however, is this observation, which

A fitting catchphrase for Acts could be, "Jesus is still doing things and teaching."

doesn't require any training in Greek: the rest of Acts confirms the idea that the church—the collection of people devoted to Jesus Christ—is a primary means (but hardly the only means) by which Jesus remains active in the world. Perhaps you've seen the promotional campaign from the United Church of Christ that declares, "God is still speaking." I love that. Inspired by that slogan and the story Acts tells, I propose that a fitting catchphrase for Acts could be, "Jesus is still doing things and teaching." He's active not in a far-off heaven but through, around, and even out in front of the church.

As we will discover in our exploration of Acts, the main way Jesus is present and active is through the Holy Spirit, which he sends to his followers (Acts 2:33) and which Acts refers to as "the Spirit of Jesus" (Acts 16:7; see also Acts 5:9; 8:39). Acts makes a big deal of the Holy Spirit, especially in the beginning chapters, and that allows readers to carry a key observation forward with them as they work through the story: Acts is about God's commitment to be present and active, transforming lives and societies. If we overlook the emphasis on the Holy Spirit and Jesus' ongoing presence in the world, we risk mistaking Acts for a celebration of the church's dauntlessness, a sappy ode to tenacity, or a suspenseful morality tale about how to survive in a difficult environment with wisdom and class. Acts has an entertaining style, and it delights in the church's endurance. But those characteristics emerge out of the book's conviction that the divine presence is on the move through, around, near, and sometimes even in spite of the believers whom Jesus sends to show and to tell his good news to others.

My clunky catchphrase—"Jesus is still doing things and teaching"—represents one way to summarize what Acts is about. As we will learn in the coming chapters, it needs some nuance. Other slogans are possible, too. Here at the outset, however, I want to steer us away from assumptions that are unhelpful. For example, some church leaders and Sunday school curriculum-makers have saddled Acts with the label *the history of the first Christians*, which makes the book sound deathly boring before you even start reading. Let Acts be as wild as the story it tells. It describes Jesus Christ, active through the Holy Spirit, continuing his work of liberating people from all kinds of oppression and alienation. It's just that now, Jesus, having risen from the dead and ascended in glory, does it in different ways than he did in Luke.

Why explore Acts now?

Acts recounts stories about events involving some of Jesus' followers during roughly the years 30–64. Acts itself was written much later, near the end of the first century, probably fifty to sixty-five years after Jesus' death and resurrection. At that time most if not all of Jesus' twelve original apostles were dead, some of them for decades. Jesus had not returned, even though many believers had assumed he would during the first generation of the church's existence. Congregations were dealing with changes in their own membership and figuring out how to replace former leaders with new ones. A revolt initiated in Judea and the surrounding area in the year 66 had been effectively put down by the Roman military in the year 70, sending shockwaves through parts of the Roman Empire and fueling suspicion and resentment toward Jewish communities. The books in the New Testament as we know it today had not been widely circulated, and several of them did not yet exist. In this context, the author of Acts wrote the book.

Acts is, of course, a narrative. To help the church in a period of transition and possible confusion, the author did not write a sermon to reinvigorate congregations. Nor a treatise to explain core Christian teachings. Nor a handbook on effective ministry or church organization. Remember, Acts relates stories from the early generations of the Christian movement, but it doesn't do so for nostalgia's sake or to make sure every congregation had a definitive record of facts and figures. Acts is not that kind of literature. Rather, Acts describes episodes and people from the young church's history so that communities of believers near the end of the first century would know who they were. Acts tells its stories so Christians would remember what God had called them to do and how God had been faithful so far. Remembering the past is a way to equip yourself for the future, especially when you look back in time with an unshakable assurance that God was at work then.

We don't know exactly how well Acts did its job back in the first century. People saved, reproduced, and circulated the book, so that's a sign that something worked. Apparently, the author of Acts was not the only one convinced that God had been accompanying the church in its early years.

I teach and write about Acts frequently. One reason is because I enjoy a challenge that sparks a good amount of scholarly research about Acts: trying to discover how ancient Christian audiences might have understood Acts and why they might have turned to it to help them contend with questions they expected their faith to answer. Another reason, which explains why I wrote this book, is because I'm interested in seeing how Acts equips congregations and individuals today to move forward. In other words, my scholarship usually focuses on what Acts has meant in the past. This book pays attention to those issues, but it's also interested in a different question: how should Christians engage Acts as we journey into the future?

I've described Acts as a wild and challenging book that can expand imaginations about God and the transformative potential of God's good news. In an era when many congregations are anxious about aging memberships, shifting demographics, and diminished cultural influence, Acts might reorient perspectives. In a period when many churches resist change, value rules more than grace, suffer from toxic ideologies that wreck Christianity's moral credibility, and feel pressure to become more withdrawn or sectarian, Acts might cause us to notice new ways in which God makes the good news known through generosity, inclusion, and a willingness to offer bold or countercultural expressions of our faith in Jesus Christ. In a time when some congregations have stopped believing they have a future, Acts says: *remember where you came from.*

When I study Acts with students, pastors, and laypeople, I'm consistently reminded that Acts is not as one-dimensional as I sometimes presume. I also notice again and again that my own cultural perspectives and privileges—especially those afforded to me as an educated straight white man in American society—affect what I detect in Acts. As a teacher, I must regularly commit myself to learn from others who might be much more or less comfortable than I am with a passage from Acts. I need to be in conversation with a variety of perspectives. That keeps me aware that remembering "where you came from" is never about utter uniformity or going back to a monocultural church (which never existed in the first century, anyway). As we will see, Acts is very comfortable with communities of believers in which every member brings his or her own self to the table. I suggest, then, that you bring your own self to Acts and eventually also seek out ways to learn from what other readers see in it.

As with any book in the Bible, Acts has its problematic parts, and parts of Acts have been used in problematic ways. We will discuss several examples in the chapters ahead. The story occasionally adopts a hostile attitude toward some people it views as opponents. It neglects to describe the faithful activities of many believers in the ancient church, especially slaves and women. Its imprecise characterization of certain Jewish groups has made it a resource for antisemitism. It sometimes makes harmonious existence within Christian congregations look almost effortless. I'm positive that Acts remains a powerful story, but that doesn't mean we sweep the difficult aspects under the rug or refuse to correct harmful ways it has been used.

Getting everyone to read Acts won't save the world, or the church. But learning to read Acts well will help us get into a beneficial frame of mind. The big, plucky, and occasionally wild story of Acts celebrates the new possibilities that spring into being when Jesus' followers start to come to grips with the wonder of an empty tomb and the fiery initiative of God's Holy Spirit. Acts asks the church to be daring—not necessarily heroic—in response. People become daring in Acts because they open themselves to what the presence of the Holy Spirit represents: new life and a new society. The Holy Spirit, the presence of Jesus, heralds the arrival of God's salvation and the world's liberation. Those who are led by the Spirit therefore open themselves up to a new normal—

a world in which the old limits, injustices, strife, and rivalries start to become undone.[1]

I have a deep appreciation for humanity's penchant to make mistakes or to be utterly clueless. So I enjoy the fact that believers in Acts are routinely surprised by the Holy Spirit or required to figure out (or catch up with) what the Spirit is doing. They are travelers, not just across the miles of the Roman Empire, but across trails the Spirit is blazing. They often need help. Is the same Spirit that animated the churches of the first century still shining to beckon a way forward? Do lessons learned about the Spirit in the past urge Christians today to encounter God and share God's goodness in solidarity with the wider world? Can we still discover the Spirit among us? If you want to answer those questions, reading Acts will give you the language and imagination to get started.

> **B**elievers in Acts are routinely surprised by the Holy Spirit or required to figure out (or catch up with) what the Spirit is doing.

Overview of Acts

If you're able to read all of Acts before you go much further in this book, that will help you keep your mind wrapped around the big picture as we explore individual passages. Even if that will be the very first time you've ever read Acts, this book is designed to be a reliable guide for you into the story.

---

1 This description is based on my article "Preaching Acts in Easter (Year A)," Working Preacher, April 6, 2017, https://www.workingpreacher.org/craft.aspx?post=4853.

Acts begins with Jesus, after his resurrection, saying farewell to his followers near Jerusalem. From that point forward, those followers, who make up the community that will become known as the church, become the central protagonists of the story. Some of them are apostles (which comes from the Greek word *apostolos*, meaning ambassador, delegate, or envoy), whom Jesus selected in Luke 6:12-16. Most of them are other followers, whom we might identify with the generic term *believers*. Once everyone in the overall group receives the Holy Spirit ten days after Jesus' departure they take all sorts of opportunities to tell other people about the good news. They remain in Jerusalem at first, where Peter is the most prominent person in the story. In time, once it becomes dangerous for the group to remain conspicuous in Jerusalem, the narrative follows individuals as they venture to neighboring lands. Stephen, Philip, and Barnabas are three members of the church who stand out in certain scenes.

Eventually a man named Saul finds himself transformed and joins the church. Within a few chapters he and Barnabas become the focus of the story as they travel around the northeastern edges of the Mediterranean Sea. Eventually Saul, who becomes known as Paul, separates from Barnabas and travels with other associates to a number of cities to continue his ministry. When he returns to Jerusalem he is arrested and held in Roman custody until the end of the book. Before Acts concludes, however, he manages to get himself transferred to Rome, the heart of the Roman Empire.

Acts covers a lot of ground. In other words, the action takes us into many regions across the vast Roman-controlled landscape. The geographic scope of the book is wider than any other writing in the New Testament. If it feels to you like Acts thinks the good news matters for the whole known world (at least, the world viewed from a Roman perspective), you're right. Along with the range of geography is a relatively wide cultural variety. Acts depicts the challenges of making the good news understandable in an array of local cultures with all their idiosyncrasies.

Even with all the characters and settings, Acts tells only a small part of a larger story about the experiences of Christian churches in the first century. The narrative focuses almost exclusively on men; for some reason Acts is hardly interested in highlighting women's significant contributions to the vitality of the early church. Acts also keeps readers' attention on only a small number of the apostles and very few other believers. It is not a comprehensive book, in terms of telling all that might have been told about the first generations of believers.

It's common for people to read Acts and express a desire to know about the people and events that Acts does not discuss. Those are important topics, and by the time you reach the end of this book you'll be in a good position to understand what's missing and expand your insights into Acts to find evidence of several untold stories lurking between the lines. Acts can't keep everyone hidden.

Although we began with Acts 1:1-2, we will not walk through Acts in sequence from start to finish. Instead, in six chapters we will explore six different themes or ways of looking at the action in Acts by dipping our toes into a few passages I've selected. None of my chapters is exhaustive, meaning that it's impossible to consider every relevant scene from Acts without making the chapters too long. The point of the format I've chosen for this book is to help you get used to Acts and to make you ready to wade deeper into its wild story on your own. There's a lot happening in the pages of Acts. Stay alert for ways that the story's portrayal of a Spirit-led church resonates with you, clashes with your experiences, or challenges you to expand your outlook. Most of all, enjoy the ride.

<h1 style="text-align:right">Chapter 1</h1>

What God Has Done

Passages to explore

» Acts 1:3-11	Jesus' final words and promises to his followers
» Acts 2:1-36	Peter's speech in Jerusalem during Pentecost
» Acts 3:11-26	Peter's speech in Solomon's Portico in Jerusalem
» Acts 13:13-43	Paul's speech in the synagogue in Pisidian Antioch
» Acts 17:16-34	Paul's speech to the Areopagus in Athens

Whenever a new *Star Wars* movie comes out or I get ready to start watching the next season in a television show I like, I always go online to read synopses of what happened in the previous installment. In film sequels and shows, the story often picks up right where it left off, but I've had months if not a full year to get distracted by other things. I forgot what I used to know about who's a Jedi, which of the kids from Hawkins might still be possessed by the Mind Flayer, and whether Piper and Alex were officially a couple the last time I saw them. What crisis needs to be resolved? What's supposed to happen next? What did I learn from the story so far?

When we start reading our way through Acts, we need to be aware that it begins with unresolved confusion, excitement, and expectation hanging in the air. We might say the story, as a continuation of Luke's Gospel, assumes its readers are still up to speed with everything. Jesus is still with his friends, having been raised from the dead to their great surprise. He defeated death—a rather climactic aspect of the plot! Maybe we remember that throughout Luke he spoke about the arrival of the "kingdom of God." If we reread the final verses in the Gospel we will notice that Jesus talks about "repentance and forgiveness of sins" for "all nations" and "power from on high" about to come to his disciples (Luke 24:46–49).

As Acts gets rolling, Jesus commissions his followers to perform a task: they will bear witness about him. They will have to communicate what God has shown them through all they experienced during their time with Jesus.

In other words, they are going to spread the Christian message. They are going to convey God's good news. We don't know if they're eager or frightened at the beginning of Acts, but certainly they're being called into action. They witnessed a stunning transformation—their friend who was executed by Roman officials was raised to new life—and so their lives have changed. After experiencing something like that, their whole conception of what's normal and what's possible must also be transforming. What are they going to tell people? What exactly has God done? What is this new Christian message, after all?

In this opening chapter we will explore several passages that sketch the contours of the Christian message, as Acts presents it to readers. The passages I'll set before us are mostly scenes in which a prominent member of the church offers a speech or sermon to an assembled crowd. We need to remember, however, that speeches are not the only way Acts communicates what the good news is and what changes it sets in motion.

The thirteenth-century friar Saint Francis of Assisi said, "It is no use walking anywhere to preach unless our walking is our preaching." (He's popularly quoted as having declared, "Preach the gospel at all times; when necessary, use words," but that saying never appears in his writings.) Francis urged his followers to pursue consistency in how they lived and what they said. Acts is reaching for something similar, I think, because it is a story about the communities that believers form together and the deeds believers perform on behalf of their neighbors, just as much as it is a story about the message believers speak aloud to others. Passages we will explore in future chapters in this book will help us appreciate this even more.

If you belong to a church that recites creeds in worship, such as the Apostles' or the Nicene Creed, or that subscribes to certain "confessions of faith" (my church does both), you might assume that the topic "what God has done" has to involve a long list or explain complicated theological topics. That's not true for Acts. For the most part, Acts is interested in making one basic point about God's activity: God has made Jesus the source and guarantee of humanity's salvation.

As we will see shortly, Acts affirms that Jesus is the Christ, the one God sent to fulfill God's promises to the people of Israel and the whole world. Often Acts emphasizes Jesus' resurrection as a decisive moment in which his identity as Savior and Lord was vindicated by God. His resurrection means more than a reversal of fortune or a second chance at life; it is

> For the most part, Acts is interested in making one basic point about God's activity: God has made Jesus the source and guarantee of humanity's salvation.

the declaration that God wields power over death itself. No form of captivity to anything like death, ignorance, illness, or satanic influence can withstand the liberating power of God. Jesus' resurrection and ascension have declared that. Moreover, those events have accomplished that liberation, altering the makeup of all creation. For God has now installed Jesus Christ, the resurrected one, as judge over humanity and made him the reason why we are released from our sins' power and why people will be raised to new life after their own deaths.

Nowhere does anyone in Acts provide a detailed explanation of exactly *how* Jesus brings God's salvation into its fullness in all those ways, but repeatedly people in Acts insist *that* Jesus does so. Accordingly, many of the speeches in Acts draw attention to Jesus Christ's unique authority and the confident hope that humanity can expect resurrection from the dead. Different speeches will use different language and highlight different details because every speech has its own audience and its own circumstances that make the speech necessary in the first place. The speakers in Acts don't bear witness to Jews in exactly the same way as to Gentiles. Hostile audiences hear about the good news differently than friendly audiences do. All of that makes sense. There's a good reason why preachers' funeral sermons aren't exactly the same as the sermons they give during the annual stewardship drive.

What has God done? Acts can't fully answer that question. Or it won't fully answer it. Acts just gets us started toward crafting an answer by announcing with confidence that Jesus is the fulcrum for the fulfillment of God's gracious intentions for humanity. I find this very helpful, that Acts does not lead readers into precise descriptions and theological hair-splitting. That's not the purpose of the book. Rather, Acts urges us to see how the earliest believers took that core conviction, arising from their own experiences with Jesus, and trusted it. And they shared it. And they opened themselves up to discover more and more of its implications. Acts asserts that through Jesus God changed the world and revealed the future to come. In addition Acts believes that God continues to disclose the far-reaching consequences and implications of what God has done through Jesus Christ.

As Acts begins, the experiences Jesus' followers had with him in the past generate their capacity to live into a new future, if they keep up with the Holy Spirit. The church in Acts is on several journeys: people travel to new places, and they also come to discover the boundless richness of God's salvation. Acts implies that similar discoveries remain possible for Jesus' followers today.

Acts 1:3-11

Jesus' final words and promises to his followers

If Jesus had talked to communications and marketing consultants after the original Easter Sunday I suppose their first recommendation would have been: get new apostles. The apostles, along with his other followers, fell asleep on Jesus when they were supposed to be praying (Luke 22:39-46). One of them, Peter, repeatedly denied knowing him (Luke 22:54-62). When a number of women from the larger group told them they found Jesus' corpse missing from his tomb and met two angels with a message of resurrection, they scoffed (Luke 24:1-11). Those women remind us that not everyone who had been with Jesus had such a bad track record in the reliability department, but the apostles did.

In Acts 1 the apostles might have come around a little bit since the ending of Luke, and at least they have confidence that Jesus' promises of a "kingdom" are still going to come to fruition in some way. But they're going to need help going forward. They've given no indication they can figure things out on their own. Fortunately they won't have to, because just a handful of verses into the story, Jesus renews the pledge that he will send the Holy Spirit (recalling Luke 3:16; 24:49). This Spirit, Acts will reveal over time, will empower their ability to speak and live out the good news.

"You will be my witnesses," Jesus says (Acts 1:8) before he disappears from their sight. It's not a request or even a command. It's a declaration.

In a parking garage a few years ago I witnessed someone smash her car into a parked pickup truck, pull into a nearby parking space, and run away. When I spoke to a police officer later, I told him what happened, but when he asked specific questions to gather additional details, like what the driver was wearing and whether she seemed under the influence, I found myself apologizing for not being able to offer him more. "That's OK," he said, "you can only tell me what you saw." That's what it means to be a witness, whether in a legal setting or when talking about religious faith:

we can only describe what we've experienced.

Whenever Acts talks about being a witness, bearing witness, or testifying, it's saying about the same thing the officer told me. Jesus informs his followers they will publicly recount to others the things they know to be true. In some scenes they will do that with words; in other scenes they will declare the nature of the good news through worship, prayer, care and healing, sharing meals with others, extending fellowship, expressing compassion, and generously sharing resources. Christian "witness" is at the heart of believers' activity in Acts. It involves people naming, confirming, and embodying truths that have already been manifested to them in their lived experiences with Jesus Christ. The apostles and others are not expected to possess secret knowledge or specialized abilities. As Jesus' witnesses, they will talk about him and what they have received from him. As people empowered by the Holy Spirit, they will turn out to be much more reliable than they have been in the story so far.

Acts 2:1-36

Peter's speech in Jerusalem during Pentecost

Pentecost was originally (and still is) a Jewish festival. Scripture establishes it as a celebration of the wheat harvest (Exodus 34:22; Deuteronomy 16:9-10). Because it is one of Judaism's three pilgrimage festivals, in the first century many Jews would travel to Jerusalem for the occasion. That helps explain why the Holy Spirit empowers believers to speak so many languages in the Pentecost story. The church begins its public witness in Acts with a message to people who hailed from a multitude of places—both Jews and "proselytes" (who are non-Jews who had converted to Judaism).

With hyperbole, Acts says that this Jewish crowd contains travelers and immigrants "from every nation under heaven." The Greek word for "nation" is *ethnos*. Don't equate it to modern ideas of a "nation-state" or "country." The expres-

> The church of Jesus Christ consists of a unity that gathers differences and distinctions into a common home.

sion calls attention to the variety of people who composed the diverse membership of Judaism. This notion of *ethnos*, like the English word *ethnicity*, calls attention to the factors that figure in people's understandings of their identities based on their familial, linguistic, genealogical, regional, and cultural particularities. At Pentecost the Holy Spirit directs Jesus' followers to speak first to a representative sample of all Judaism, with its wide array of differences. From that diverse group the new community that will be called "the church" attracts thousands of new members all at once.

The broad assortment of people and languages makes an important statement before Peter even starts his speech: the good news will not ultimately belong to one kind of people or one core ethnicity. That sense of a community composed of multiple identities will grow clearer later in Acts, when non-Jews (Gentiles) unite with the church. Imagine how different it might be if the Holy Spirit had prompted Jesus' followers to address the crowd only in Hebrew or Greek. Instead, all languages belong; no one gives up who they are in order to become integrated into a homogeneous church culture. Instead, variation is one of the church's original characteristics. The church of Jesus Christ consists of a unity that gathers differences and distinctions into a common home. That's a message many congregations I know need to hear.

Peter starts speaking because everyone is equally "amazed and perplexed." His speech is difficult to follow, but in essence it accomplishes three things. First, Peter interprets the dramatic events of the day as nothing less than the arrival of God's Spirit. Drawing from Joel 2:28-32, Peter says the coming of the Holy Spirit signals the beginning of "the last days," a new culminating chapter in God's history with the world. In this new era when salvation is available—very near at hand—Jesus' followers will "prophesy," which means they announce the imminence of salvation as a gift from God. The Spirit behind that power to prophesy is God's presence within and among believers of all sexes, ages, and social classes.

Second, Peter identifies Jesus as the Christ (another word for the "Messiah" or the "Anointed One") and the reason why salvation is fully available and why the Spirit of God has come. Peter explains that various Jewish scriptures bear witness to the resurrected Jesus as the Christ and the fulfillment of long-standing hopes. He appeals to sacred texts and their oblique references to someone being unharmed by death and someone ruling at God's right hand. The speech mentions God often, attributing everything about Jesus' ministry, resurrection, and enduring authority to God. For Peter, literally all facets of Jesus' life story are indications of God's involvement in that story and a demonstration of God's commitment to humanity. And now, because he has assumed his place of authority at God's right hand, the resurrected and exalted Christ has poured out the Holy Spirit.

I should pause and note that there's a lot of God-language in my previous paragraph. How are we supposed to keep God, Jesus, and the Holy Spirit all straight, and shouldn't the notion of the Trinity help sort this out? Frankly, I'm not sure that appealing to the Trinity *ever* makes things *easier* to understand. But the point is a good one—isn't Peter tying himself up in a theological knot here? Yes and no. Acts was written long before anyone proposed a doctrine of "the Trinity," and so Acts is not meticulous about differentiating among the three Divine Persons. But all of the God-language in Acts also shows us one reason why Christians eventually proposed the Trinity as a way of describing God and how we come to know God, since in this passage and elsewhere Acts mentions intertwined relationships among the actions of God, Jesus Christ, and the Holy Spirit. The bottom line for Peter's Pentecost speech is this: it's all about God—from the old promises in ancient Israel's history, to the recent events involving Jesus of Nazareth, to the recently arrived Holy Spirit, and to all that the Spirit will make possible.

Third and finally, Peter entreats his audience to embrace what he has just told them so they too can experience freedom from sins and the presence of the Holy Spirit. He calls them to "repent"—to change their minds about Jesus—and to "be baptized." There are no conditions that might hold them back. I imagine he spreads his arms wide when he states, "The promise is for you and for your children and for all who are far off, everyone whom the Lord our God calls" (Acts 2:39 ESV).

In other words, everything has changed. For everyone.

Acts 3:11-26

Peter's speech in Solomon's Portico in Jerusalem

Right on the heels of the first speech in Acts (at Pentecost), Acts describes the first healing performed by apostles

(Acts 3:1-10). Calling on Jesus' power as he speaks of Jesus' "name," Peter helps a man who was never able to walk stand up and enter a portion of the Temple called Solomon's Portico. This demonstration of authority over a lifelong incapacitating condition attracts the attention of a flabbergasted crowd. So Peter bears witness about Jesus, naming him as the unseen source of the man's newfound wholeness and also attesting to the power of faith in him.

Jesus possesses this power that works through the apostles because of God. God raised "the Author of life" from the dead and "glorified" (that is, bestowed honored upon) him. The detailed references to the circumstances of Jesus' death are curious, because Peter addresses this crowd as if they are exactly the same ones who turned their backs on Jesus in the presence of the Roman governor Pontius Pilate in Luke 23:13-25. Peter isn't confused, though. He speaks as if responsibility for Jesus' execution extends widely, almost as if that culpability belongs to everyone associated with Jerusalem or if it is simply part of the human condition, from God's perspective. At the same time, forgiveness and refreshment extend widely, too, and so Peter invites everyone to get ready for the "universal restoration" (literally, in Greek: "the restoration of all people" or "the restoration of all things") that God is prepared to make a reality.

The point where Peter mentions "universal restoration" is one of the places where I wish Acts was a little longer. If only Peter's sermon included just a couple additional sentences to explain what he means by that expression. It does not appear anywhere else in the New Testament, so there are questions about what exactly Peter has in mind. At least he refers to the prophets, so presumably some of the Old Testament's prophetic writings' most grandiose hopes are in view here. Imagine the visions the prophets tried to convey. Visions of justice extended to those who continually suffer injustice. Visions of all people enjoying everlasting security. Visions of shalom, a situation of peace, health, and abundance established by God. Peter also mentions the offspring of Abraham who will provide blessing to all of the world's families (recalling Genesis 22:18; 26:4). That offspring is Jesus, and Peter's comment reiterates that the "universal restoration" will include more than Jews alone. The scope and scale of this good news is immense.

I occasionally have to remind students not to fault the Bible for failing to give precise descriptions of what the future will look like when God has finished constructing it. All language, metaphors, and images are bound to fall short. Maybe the point of the ambiguity is to call our imaginations into action. Some of the Bible's attempts to portray aspects of God's restorative work are pretty good fuel for Spirit-filled dreamers. Consider, for example, Isaiah 65:17-25, which speaks about considerably increased lifespans and wolves and lambs eating alongside one another with none of them looking over their shoulder. Directed by prophetic visions like those, let your imagination about the restoration God has promised run wild.

Acts 13:13-43

Paul's speech in the synagogue in Pisidian Antioch

When Paul travels to the region of Pisidia and a nearby city called Antioch, which was an inland city in the western half of modern Turkey, he takes an opportunity to address a Jewish audience. It is the first of Paul's speeches that Acts records. He begins by swiftly summarizing the history of ancient Israel, from slavery in Egypt to the establishment of

David's kingdom. He identifies Jesus as a Savior who came from King David's lineage, which is a statement about more than genealogy. It means Jesus revives hopes for a renewal of ancient Israel's glory days, especially in the sense of freedom from oppressors and a widespread reverence for God's holiness. (The New Testament consistently remembers David for his best qualities and accomplishments, not his worst.) Paul will also say, furthermore, that Jesus the Savior is greater than David, for unlike Israel's greatest king his corpse underwent no corruption.

To understand what God has done through Jesus, Paul says, his audience of fellow Jews needs to look back further into their history. The life, execution, and resurrection of Jesus demonstrate that God is keeping promises.

I prefer it when people make me specific promises instead of general ones. That way I know when they have or haven't kept them. "I'll repay you your $50 on Thursday afternoon" is more helpful to me than "Don't worry, I'll take care of it." So exactly what promises does Paul have in mind in this speech? Although he is not especially specific about them, the overall context of the speech helps identify them. One is the promise of a Savior, someone who will lead God's people into the blessings God has in store for them. As we will see through the course of our exploration of Acts, salvation has many dimensions, including more than forgiveness of sins. Everything about salvation stems from the Savior. And Paul declares his Savior to be alive and active.

A second promise is liberation and security. Paul mentions the exodus from slavery in Egypt, the conquest of Canaan, and the emergence of King David. All of those events from the Old Testament's greatest-hits album demonstrate God's commitment to keep the people descended from Abraham safe from harm and oppression. Deliverance from enemies and damage were prominent themes also in Jesus' ministry (Luke 1:72-75; 4:16-19; see also Acts 2:40; 26:18).

The last promise to notice stems from the other two: resurrection from the dead. When God raised Jesus it was more than merely an impressive display of divine power. Paul implies that resurrection itself is the keeping of a promise, the promise that God makes life after death possible. Jewish groups in the first century were divided over the issue of whether human beings should expect an afterlife, or whether what we have now is all there is. Paul argues that God definitively settled those debates by raising Jesus from the dead. Elsewhere he refers to Jesus as "the first to rise from the dead" and goes on to explain that his resurrection confirms God's promises in the Jewish holy books of the Law and the Prophets (Acts 26:22-23; see also 23:6-8). All of scripture's grand hopes for peace, security, wholeness, prosperity, and blessing will come to pass. With Jesus' resurrection God has declared that those who have died will not miss out on any of it.

Acts 17:16-34

Paul's speech to the Areopagus in Athens

Many years ago I rode an elevator with Christie Brinkley and Billy Joel. I'm not sure they were even aware I was there. He was humming a Beatles song and she just waited for the door to reopen. But for twenty seconds *I was there*.

Maybe you have a piece of rubble from the Berlin Wall or a beloved author once autographed a book for you. We like our mental and physical souvenirs of times we had contact with noteworthy people and places. Those memories give us ways to boast without being obnoxious about it.

In a similar way, the passage about Paul in Athens is a trophy story. "Look! Our guy was *there*—in Athens, the place that symbolizes the intellectual accomplishments of the ancient Greek-speaking world. Paul spoke, and the Athenians listened." The sheer presence of this story in Acts celebrates the importance of the Christian message and Paul's rhetorical skills. Even if Acts pokes fun at the Athenians as obsessed with exchanging ideas among themselves, still this scene marks a high point in the plot.

When the local intellectuals make it possible for Paul to present his teachings to the Areopagus, the council of the city's governing authorities, he gives them a speech tailor-made for people familiar with certain Greek philosophical traditions. His audience is probably entirely Gentile, so he does not discuss Jewish scriptures. Rather, he speaks about humanity's search for the Divine and about a shared conviction that deities are not contained within temples, statues, or altars. The God Paul proclaims is close by.

Nothing Paul says in his speech would have been terribly controversial to his Greek peers until he gets to the end and declares that this nearby God has made a clear statement to the world by raising a man from the dead. That claim about Jesus' resurrection is too much for some in the audience; they ridicule him. Others want to hear more, and still others embrace the good news.

I don't think anyone can *prove* that Jesus was raised from the dead. That piece of Christian faith depends not on the tools of science, history, philosophy, or militaries but on the witness of the entire church. That testimony began in the experiences of people like Mary Magdalene, Peter, and Paul, and it is reaffirmed in our own encounters with the resurrected Christ through sacraments, personal experiences, serving others, and the word of God that we encounter in congregational life and out in the world. The message of the resurrection rarely fits humanity's ordinary ways of making sense of how the world works. That's true whether we are walking among intellectual giants or sitting with simpler folk who make their way through life with homespun wisdom.

Yet that is Paul's message for the Athenians: resurrection. As we know all too well, death is very good at its job. A huge leap of faith is required for a person to declare that death is not the end. Paul implies, moreover, that the idea of an afterlife is not something to debate as an abstract concept. His testimony, that God has spoken and given assurance to the world through the resurrection of Jesus, demands attention now, from all people. Paul insists that by resurrecting Jesus God has done more than merely reverse death. God has opened up a whole new future. God has promised to change us. God has vowed to judge the world so the result will be righteousness, which is a restored relationship between humanity and God—the Divine Being that humanity expends so much effort to find. According to Paul, God has said through Jesus, "I'm here!"

Reflections

As we continue to work through Acts I'll occasionally refer to "new things that God makes possible" or believers in Acts coming to recognize "new possibilities emerging" in their midst. The five passages we've just explored give some substance to what I mean with those expressions. Repeatedly people in Acts announce that God was active through Jesus Christ and that Jesus is the Savior who makes salvation a present reality. Everything else in the book builds on those foundational claims about God's accomplishments, including the arrival and power of the Holy Spirit to continue the good work. The entire narrative of Acts, through its stories about speeches, events, struggles, and discoveries, reaffirms the belief that God has acted and continues to act.

As the speeches of Pentecost, Solomon's Portico, and Pisidian Antioch make clear, the salvation Acts talks about is not new in the sense of "never before imagined." The Christian message derives from older Jewish convictions and hopes. The God we meet through Jesus Christ is not unknown at all but is the God of Abraham and Sarah and the God of Miriam and Moses. The good news that Peter, Paul, and others proclaim is a declaration that God has fulfilled promises that we can read about in the Jewish scriptures, which Christians call the Old Testament. What's "new" for Christians is that we believe those promises came to pass through Jesus of Nazareth and that the Holy Spirit continues to connect those promises to us.

One of the most important and humbling discoveries in my own journey of faith has been my ongoing realization of how much damage Christians have historically done to our Jewish neighbors by assuming that faith in Jesus Christ involves a radical departure from Jewish understandings of who God is and what God intends for humanity. Too many Christians commit a grave error when they suppose that our religion was the first to discover grace, justice, peace, reconciliation, and mercy residing in the heart of God. Those ideas run through the Old Testament and they form the bedrock beneath the promises that Acts has in view. If we read Acts well, we will grasp that it tells a story of God's ongoing faithfulness to Jews and their hopes as well as a story of how that faithfulness comes also to benefit Gentiles.

Likewise, if we want to understand what kind of world this generous God has in mind and what divine faithfulness looks like in action, we need to follow the story's lead and commit ourselves to examining the Old Testament. In particular, we should notice what the Old Testament longs for and what it says about the transformations and restorations that God intends for human existence. When Peter speaks of a "universal restoration" accomplished because of Jesus Christ, those ancient scriptures will activate our creativity.

Biblical scholars sometimes find Luke and Acts frustrating because those writings have an occasional habit of referring to the Old Testament in broad brushstrokes instead of highlighting specific scriptural passages. The vague reference to times of "universal restoration that God announced long ago through his holy prophets" (Acts 3:21) is one example. Another appears in Luke 24:27 when the resurrected Jesus is with two of his followers and we read: "Then beginning with Moses and all the prophets, he interpreted to them the things about himself in all the scriptures" (see also Acts 3:21, 24; 10:43; 13:27). But what I appreciate about that kind of unspecific writing is that it challenges me to think creatively. I don't think every sentence of the Old Testament is about Jesus, strictly speaking. But I do want to take Luke and Acts seriously when they say something big and culminating has occurred through Jesus Christ. Apparently, then, none of the promises I find in scripture is too outlandish to believe. Maybe wolves and lambs will indeed one day settle their differences.

The most inscrutable thing God makes possible through Jesus Christ is resurrection from the dead. When Jesus' followers have encounters with him, transformed, after his death, it changes everything for them. It makes them decide that all the great things they have hoped for as Jews in particular and as human beings in general are going to happen. Those encounters, of course, launch the Book of Acts and form the core of the church's witness about a reliable and transformative God.

I'm always puzzled by Christians who think they can confess faith in the resurrection of the dead but then behave callously toward strangers and people in need. Anyone who thinks the hope of life after death minimizes the importance of this life and the imperative to go out of one's way to preserve the dignity of other human beings has distorted Christian faith into something monstrous. In Acts, confidence in bodily resurrection does more

> In Acts, confidence in bodily resurrection does more than compel believers to speak and face their own deaths with courage; it also changes how they live and spurs them to care for others in self-sacrificial ways.

than compel believers to speak and face their own deaths with courage; it also changes how they live and spurs them to care for others in self-sacrificial ways. That way of living comes across as anything but a burden. It is part of how the church experiences the joyful benefits of God's salvation right now. As a result, it is not optional for my congregation or your congregation to do the same. Generous care and hospitality constitute a necessary part of what it means to be "witnesses" of Christ and his resurrection.

As we go forward in our exploration of Acts we will discover that the church's witness does not remain static throughout the story. There is more to talk about than what happened in the past. Not only is believers' faith focused on what God has done through Jesus Christ, it also must repeatedly reckon with God's penchant for showing up in their midst. Members of the church in Acts discover new realities as they remain responsive to the prompting of the Holy Spirit.

Chapter 2

What God Does

Passages to explore

» Acts 8:4-8, 14-17 The apostles and the Samaritan
                                     converts
» Acts 8:26-40   Philip and the Ethiopian court
                                     official
» Acts 9:1-20   Saul and Ananias
» Acts 10:1-48   Peter and Cornelius

From my children I learned about interactive books, video games, and films. These are media in which readers, gamers, and viewers control the plot and bear some responsibility for how a story proceeds and eventually ends. In the *Choose Your Own Adventure* book series, you decide how a character should respond in a situation—such as traveling through the woods or taking the long way around through the desert—and the book directs you to a new page so you can read about what happens as a result. In the *Bandersnatch* episode of the Netflix series *Black Mirror*, you interact with the movie. By pointing and clicking you direct characters to take certain actions that will have distinct outcomes, which you see as the video seamlessly jumps to show you what happens next. Decisions you make early in the plot will open up or shut down future possibilities.

Those kinds of entertainment provide lessons in cause and effect. They remind us that a single event can have all kinds of consequences, even if we can't immediately anticipate any of them. Sometimes things happen in life that have potential to change everything and to set the future on an entirely new trajectory that we discover as we travel along its path.

Of course Acts is not interactive, but it lets us experience a similar sensation of coming to discover new possibilities emerging because of events that have transpired in the past. It's fair to say that all of Acts proceeds from the conviction that the whole world changes—and our entire conception of "what's possible" changes—as a consequence of Jesus' life, death, resurrection, ascension, and gift of the Holy Spirit. God has defeated death. God dwells among God's people and all the world through the Holy Spirit. "The time of universal restoration" (Acts 3:21) is at hand. Everything that happens next is influenced by that past.

Then, additional consequences and realities continue to manifest themselves as Acts progresses. It's a story of the Spirit choosing an adventure for Jesus' followers. At the beginning of Acts they don't receive a map of the entire plot that will unfold before them, but they are told the role they will play: empowered by the Holy Spirit, they will be Jesus' "witnesses in Jerusalem, in all Judea and Samaria, and to the ends of the earth" (Acts 1:8). As long as they continue to bear witness, they will be surprised. They will discover that the God of resurrection power has much in store for them and the wider world. Their comprehension of the lived, experienced implications of the good news will suddenly expand.

The best examples of people realizing those expansion moments in Acts are stories of dramatic and unexpected conversions, when people who are truly unusual

> Acts presents these stories to readers as about much more than increased church membership or individuals "getting saved." The stories also involve the broader church discovering God's activity among them.

(in the best sense of that word) hear the good news and enter into fellowship with other followers of Jesus Christ. Acts presents these stories to readers as about much more than increased church membership or individuals "getting saved." The stories also involve the broader church discovering God's activity among them.

Everyone involved in these stories—not just the "converts"—experiences change. God opens up new vistas for the church's work and imagination. What no one thought possible yesterday becomes not only possible today but utterly game-changing tomorrow. That's what God does, according to how Acts perceives life in the post-Easter world. God's activity is described as people coming to grasp new understandings of how extensive God's salvation is. Believers discover the Holy Spirit on the move out in front of the church, urging them to follow and grow. When the church catches up, it is amazed. And changed.

Acts 8:4-8, 14-17

The apostles and the Samaritan converts

Jesus informed his followers that they would be his witnesses in Samaria, but up until Acts 8 none of them seems to have tried or wanted to go there. It takes the onset of persecution, which made remaining in Jerusalem unsafe, to compel anyone to travel about forty miles to the north and start talking to Samaritans (Acts 8:1, 5).

I can understand the hesitation, because the Samaritans were among the last people that many Judean and Galilean Jews would have wanted to socialize with, let alone share good news with. From the Jews' perspective the Samaritans were descendants of Hebrews from the ancient Northern Kingdom of Israel who long ago had married people from other nations and therefore forfeited God's blessings. They were false claimants to the identity "the people of God." As far as the Samaritans were concerned, however, they were the true descendants of Abraham. The two groups made essentially the same claim about themselves as God's uniquely chosen people but had their own holy texts, temples, and rituals. There was a history of the groups committing violence, vandalism, and sacrilege against one another.

That deep legacy of enmity appears not to be a stumbling block for Philip, however. He just goes to Samaria, delivers people from illness and demonic power, and tells everyone that Jesus is the Christ. As a result, the Samaritans go all in.

Philip was not one of the twelve apostles. (We will learn more about where he came from in the next chapter, when we will explore Acts 6.) That doesn't make anyone concerned about the validity of his actions, but there is something peculiar about what happens when he is with the Samaritans. Or, rather, what doesn't happen: the Samaritans don't receive the Holy Spirit even though they are baptized in Jesus' name. So the apostles Peter and John make the journey northward, pray for the Samaritans, lay their hands on them, and—*voilà!*—the Holy Spirit arrives.

The response this story usually generates among Christian audiences (especially the Mainline Protestants I hang out with) is: "Wait . . . what on earth just happened?" A lot of us are uncomfortable with the idea that certain church leaders and not others might be empowered with the ability to dictate exactly where God's Spirit may or may not go.

One reason we are uncomfortable is because *this kind of thing never happens just like this anywhere else in Acts.* In several scenes we witness connections between baptism, the arrival of the Spirit, and the laying on of hands, but the connections are different in almost every setting. And nowhere else is there a suggestion that one's baptism needs an extra apostolic jolt in order to become complete. If something in the story is clearly an aberration, don't build rules and doctrines around it. Instead, ask: what might explain the aberration?

Here's a hint: it's Samaria.

If anyone might seem unqualified or unworthy to join the young church of Jesus Christ, it's probably the Samaritans. Remember that on Pentecost in Acts 2 the coming of the Holy Spirit seemed to herald the fulfillment of God's intentions for all Jews, wherever their homeland and whatever their specific ethnic markers. Samaritans were not mentioned.

The Samaritans' receptivity to the good news and the willingness of God to dwell within Samaritan people would have emphatically reconfigured many Jews' notions of who this new, emerging "church" was for in the first place. That's why it's important for apostles from Jerusalem to come to Samaria, so they can experience in person the new thing that God is doing. God doesn't need Peter and John to come and grant their approval. Peter and John need to come so they, as representatives of the Jerusalem church, can know that Judeans, Galileans, and Samaritans all possess the same Holy Spirit and therefore are included together in a new, diverse community centered in Jesus Christ. God has no plans to build a special "Samaritan church" and a separate church for Jews. Peter and John are so convinced of this that when they finally journey back to Jerusalem they don't rush or go in a straight line; they go "proclaiming the good news to many villages of the Samaritans" (Acts 8:25).

I would have enjoyed being in the room to overhear when the apostles first received the message from Philip: "Please send someone to Samaria. God's at work here. Amazing stuff is happening. We need you." Maybe Peter and John's response was "Did he say *Samaria?* Oh no. Why didn't he travel west instead?" Or maybe they were overjoyed. In any case, they would have recognized that the developments in Samaria affect them, too. They have new siblings now. If Samaritans are really "in," that changes things, such as the way believers in Jerusalem talk about certain people, whom they will share holidays with, whom their children will marry, and how they will pray and worship as a gathered church.

The conversions among the Samaritans are the first of several watershed developments in Acts in which believers discover that God is moving them beyond any confined understanding of what "the church" is supposed to be. Subsequent passages will make the point even more clearly.

Acts 8:26-40

Philip and the Ethiopian court official

Philip's work is not finished. After his time in Samaria he plays a part in what I believe is the wildest scene in Acts. The story is extraordinary in nearly every way, beginning with an angel telling Philip where to go and ending with the Spirit oddly translocating him to a different place.

Everything that happens in between on a wilderness road is peculiar, too. Philip meets someone unlike anyone else in Acts: a traveler returning to a land south of Egypt, probably Meroe. He is a Nubian queen's chief treasurer. We can assume he has access to great wealth and influence, made even clearer by his possession of two expensive items: a scroll and chariot.

Acts identifies him as a eunuch, which raises questions. While that could be just a general term to describe any court official, more likely it means he has been castrated. Perhaps this was the sacrifice he had to make if he wanted to work in proximity to the queen and her household. The decision could have been made for him, however, if he was a slave or a young man handed over to the queen as tribute from a conquered people. No matter the reason for his castration, it would have opened him up to mockery and contempt from most ancient people's perspectives. According the dominant view in Greco-Roman culture, he was no longer a man.

Acts treats him as strange in numerous ways. The term *Ethiopian* might have made audiences in the Roman Empire think of exoticism. Some Romans viewed Ethiopia as the edge of the civilized world and regarded its residents as pleasant curiosities—beautiful yet mysterious. The Roman fascination with Ethiopia was a blend of wonder, ignorance, and xenophobia.

All in all, according to ancient norms the court official does not fit neatly into the boxes people use to sort one another. He enjoys some forms of power and respect but lacks others. He is neither male nor female. He may be Jewish or well acquainted with Judaism since he has been to the Temple and is reading a prophetic book, but he is very much a stranger from Philip's point of view. He and Philip can start from the same ground with a conversation about Isaiah 53:7-8, but at the same time if anyone in Acts represents the concept of *outsider* and "the ends of the earth" to which the message about Jesus will go, it's this court official.

As the passage ends, a conversion occurs. Readers should take from that event a clear and gripping statement that the good news is for everyone; there are no barriers nor advantages arising from national identity, sexual identity, social standing, or public honor. Even if there were, good luck trying to figure out where this character fits into those categories. He doesn't need to.

This story is so unusual, with so many convenient coincidences and such heavy-handed divine guidance, that I used to find it more amusing than meaningful. My reaction to the story probably made it too convenient for me to diminish the queen's treasurer as an oddity or a humorous diversion. That was a mistake. My outlook changed for two reasons.

The first was a discovery of how important this passage is for people who have been denied power, dignity, and a place at the table in Christian history. I once was asked to teach a Bible study for a group of preachers from congregations composed of Sudanese immigrants. When they found out that Acts is one of my research interests, the room lit up and they wanted to talk to me about this passage and nothing else. The court official was for them as close as one could get to a "patron saint." Christian traditions have remembered him as an evangelist who started churches in Sudan and Ethiopia. Almost twenty centuries later, he remained a direct link to the Bible for a roomful of Sudanese believers. Through him, they experienced inclusion within the stories scripture tells.

Ancient biases obviously influenced the characterization of the eunuch in Acts. Those biases are both understandable and deserving of criticism. At the same time, they appear so starkly in Acts that they make the man a powerful representative of numerous groups that have been labeled outsiders. For example, the eunuch has been for many sexual minorities both a reminder of their historic mistreatment and a dignified symbol of their certain belonging among God's people.

That leads me to the second reason why my appreciation for this story has increased. I realized how significant it is that Acts does not relay what Philip says to the Ethiopian once their theological conversation begins. He tells him the good news about Jesus; that's all we know. The Ethiopian, however, shares a theological insight that readers overhear. When he and Philip stumble upon water he says, "What is to prevent me from being baptized?" It's a rhetorical question. Everyone knows the answer is "nothing." He is not a passive convert being processed or integrated. He is a new sibling in Christ who can actively discern what God has made possible: there is a place for him in this new community that the Holy Spirit has brought into existence. He may be new to the story but he knows right away where it's headed.

The court official has perceived the implications of the good news for him. He knows: *if* God is indeed as generous and welcoming as Philip has said . . . and *if* Jesus Christ really testifies to God's presence among those who suffer harm and alienation . . . and *if* the Holy Spirit is enabling the good news to become a reality for all people in all places . . . *then* surely he, the apparent outsider, belongs.

Acts 9:1-20
Saul and Ananias

Acts introduces Saul as a quintessential villain. He appears in Acts 7:54–8:3 when a mob kills a believer named Stephen and Saul approves of the bloodshed. Saul becomes the chief figure in the wave of persecution that leaves many in the church under arrest or fleeing into surrounding regions. When he returns to the narrative spotlight in Acts 9, it's because he has approval to go to Damascus, in Syria, to apprehend believers there, too.

What happens to Saul is one of the most famous stories in Acts. With other New Testament stories it has prompted "was blind but now I see" motifs. Countless artists have painted Saul stunned on the ground (although often lying next to his horse, even though Acts makes no reference to a mount). Johnny Cash embellishes the story in his "Man in White" song, yet I confess I'm a bigger fan of "Man in Black."

Saul's world turns upside down. He begins the scene full of power and charged with leading people to Jerusalem in chains. He ends the scene unable to see and led by the hand to Damascus. His experience on the road allows him to get something right, for he responds to Jesus as "Lord," but then Jesus replies that persecuting believers is equivalent to persecuting him. The church's archenemy has been brought low.

People speak of having a Road-to-Damascus moment, in which the truth strikes them with great clarity or in which they come to know Jesus in a new way. Saul's story entails that but also includes a different kind of experience, one that can be just as shocking: a Go-to-Straight-Street moment.

That is the moment Ananias must have. He is one of the disciples in Damascus whom Saul was coming to apprehend. Like prophets in the Old Testament such as Moses and Jeremiah, Ananias is minding his own business when the Lord calls him to perform a task. Again like those prophets, Ananias offers reasons why it's a bad idea. Doesn't Jesus know who Saul is?

Ananias's response is perfectly reasonable. Saul, with all of his threats and murder, is the last person in the world a Christian disciple wants to meet face-to-face. That's when Jesus does more than reassure Ananias; he also tells him that Saul is being transformed. No longer is Saul a persecutor, for Jesus has renamed him a chosen instrument. Jesus decides who people really are; their reputations do not.

If the sole point of Jesus' confrontation of Saul on the road was to get Saul to switch teams, then this story could have been half the length. Because Ananias plays a role, there must be more going on here. If Jesus is powerful enough to generate a bright light, blind Saul, and speak with a disembodied voice, then surely Jesus is also capable of telling Saul directly all the things he told Ananias to tell Saul. So why is Ananias necessary?

He's necessary because Saul is not only being brought out of something (his old ways and understandings). He's also being brought into something (a new identity woven into the communal existence of Jesus' church). For one thing, no believer in Damascus, Jerusalem, or anywhere in between is going to trust that Saul has changed. Ananias can help with that. For another—more weighty—thing, Saul's transformation needs to be acknowledged by the people of God as an act of God. If an enemy like Saul can be turned around, potentially anyone can. Starting with Ananias, the church needs to know that.

If I were Ananias, I suppose I would make the journey to Straight Street out of a willingness to be obedient and a desire to avoid being struck blind myself. I probably would put my hands on Saul, like Jesus instructs Ananias to do. It would be difficult for me to do one additional thing that Ananias does, however: he addresses him as "Brother Saul." He looks at Saul, once the ravager of the church, and greets him as family.

If the church's comforting messages about new life, forgiveness, reconciliation, hope, and community are true for anyone, they must also be true for Saul. His transformation is an implication of the good news that no one saw coming. It's a possibility made reality. Our conventional ways of assessing people and circumstances often hold us back from embracing Jesus' efforts to reconfigure our outlook. It's easier to talk about the new possibilities the good news brings into being than it is to live into them wholeheartedly like Ananias does. That takes a willingness to risk and to love.

Acts 10:1-48
Peter and Cornelius

Despised religious rivals like the Samaritans? Check. Someone who represents dominant and degrading stereotypes of "those people" who live at the edges of civilized society like an Ethiopian eunuch? Check. A repugnant persecutor like Saul? Check. How about a Gentile (non-Jew) who is a commander in the occupying military? Well, maybe no one has thought that far ahead yet. And then we reach Acts 10.

Some people have foreseen this next pivotal step, however. In Luke 2:32, a man named Simeon saw the infant Jesus and declared God's salvation would prove to be "a light for revelation to the Gentiles." After his resurrection, Jesus told his friends that they would proclaim "repentance and forgiveness of sins" to "all nations" (Luke 24:47). Ananias learned that Saul would bring Jesus' name to "Gentiles and kings" (Acts 9:15). Apparently, no one wanted to make the first move in the Gentiles' direction, though. So God does.

Acts takes a long time to tell the story of Cornelius's conversion, probably because it means to emphasize that it takes a while for the participants to figure out what is going on. They keep repeating pieces of the story, drawing others into the work of interpreting what is happening and why Peter is supposed to go to Cornelius. Everyone seems aware that God is behind things, from Cornelius encountering an angel to Peter's vision of numerous animals. But what is God doing?

Not until the thirty-fourth verse in Acts 10, when Peter declares, "I truly understand that God shows no partiality," do the pieces start to fall into place. God has apparently repealed regulations about kosher food, for the sheet full of critters Peter previously saw while in a trance included some species forbidden by the law of Moses. The vision declares no distinction among animals in terms of their purity. Also God has told Peter to come to Cornelius and receive hospitality from a Gentile without fear of defiling himself in any way. Long-standing boundaries that Peter had internalized since his childhood are suddenly no longer in force. Peter declares God does not play favorites and does not consider any group more worthy or pure than others.

That realization alone is a major breakthrough. Everything that follows seems to pour out naturally, like torrents bursting through a broken dam to water a wide valley. Peter offers a short summary of the story of Jesus, but he can't finish his sermon before God interrupts him, as the Holy Spirit fills all the family and friends Cornelius assembled. It's one of many scenes in which an apostle has little control over what God chooses to do.

By ceasing his sermon, baptizing the group, and remaining as Cornelius's guest for several days, Peter acknowledges that the Gentiles in the house are, as of that moment, full members of the community of faith. Nothing else needs to happen to make them worthy of the name *Christian* or worthy to share space and hospitality with Peter and his Jewish associates. How does Peter know this? Because he recognizes that God has bestowed these Gentiles with the same Holy Spirit that indwells him and all the other Jewish believers.

Everything changes when Peter determines that the same Holy Spirit resides in both groups. On one hand, Peter's act of recognition is beautifully simple. It's all he needs to know to conclude that the Gentiles' admission into the family of God through Jesus Christ is a divine undertaking and now complete. On the other hand, his act stuns me because it looks too simplistic and therefore too risky. He displays a remarkable willingness to believe and to let go. I'd be more suspicious that someone was faking something. Or I'd recommend forming a commission to study this new thing for three years before making a decision. People like me come onto the scene later, in Acts 11 and 15, eager to revisit, discuss, and argue the issue. We'll explore them later, in the next chapter.

Maybe it goes without saying that Peter's initial impulse after the Holy Spirit's arrival, to welcome the Gentiles into full fellowship *as Gentiles*, became the church's position for the long haul. Christians continue to fight battles over this issue and to provide helpful nuance, but the basic belief set down in this story is that there are no qualitative differences among various kinds of Christians. No one group enjoys an inherent advantage over another. The church doesn't have a minor league team or a remedial class.

Something about Acts I find magnetic is its storytelling techniques—certain turns of phrase, foreshadowing, and use of repetition. In this story, repetition has a theological purpose. What I mean is the retelling of Cornelius and Peter's experiences has a way of modeling how we should talk about God. Different people tell their stories to one another: "This is what happened to me, now tell me again what happened to you." Conclusions about God flow out of the conversations, as people compare and consider what they've learned from one another. In the end, things start to make sense only when the action's over. It's not until the end of the story when Peter finally can put it all together from the beginning.

In my experience, life is like that. You'll never hear me ask the question, "What do you think God is up to now, in your life and surroundings?" I think it's valuable to reflect on that topic, but I also think most answers to the question are bound to be incomplete and presumptuous, if not downright self-serving. Also the question tends to assume that God's "activity" in the world is like a puppeteer pulling strings. It's easier for me instead to look back on situations, after the fact, and wonder. With the help of hindsight, I might perceive ways in which I was open or closed to God's presence in the past, and maybe I can determine what I learned about God and myself in the process. I need to hear other people's perspectives, and I need to let the tightly bound complexities of life unfold a little. We do well to remember that Acts was written long after Peter's death; the book doesn't pretend to be a record of utterly crystal-clear insights emerging in real time.

Another way the intricacies unfold in this story is through hospitality. Acts doesn't depict the conversion as a penitent change of heart or the sudden emergence of a new religious state of mind. It's about being brought into close fellowship—fellowship with God through the arrival of the Spirit, and fellowship with other believers through Peter and Cornelius's willingness to share space, food, and friendship. Once again, the conversion of a single person has repercussions for the wider church.

Reflections

An air of excitement breathes through these four transformation stories. Acts presents them as astounding and celebratory, complete with experiences that don't happen every day. That turns off some readers, because it makes them experience Acts as inaccessible or propaganda-driven. When I hear those opinions, I answer back that maybe Acts is as interested in inspiring or entertaining its readers as it is anything else. If so, that shouldn't reduce its value as scripture. It speaks to how Acts can shake up readers who may have grown sleepy or discouraged.

Acts invigorates imaginations. Imaginations are one of our best tools for asking and answering our "what if?" questions about our faith. What if enemies can really become allies? What if strangers can teach us things about God that we haven't discerned ourselves? What if God really values my neighbors—all of them—as highly as God values me? As I have mentioned, many parts of Acts lead us to expect big things from God and to discover new possibilities becoming realities. Usually when those discoveries happen, the Holy Spirit is illuminating the way.

My most influential teacher likes to point out that several of these conversion stories involve multiple conversions. For example, Cornelius undergoes a conversion but so does Peter, in terms of his understanding of how his own life and values must change once God's Spirit falls upon Gentiles. Ananias's view of Saul and what's possible for him undergoes a renovation. Because of the Samaritan's conversion, the Jerusalem church understands itself differently, for now its members are united to the Samaritans. Old assumptions must go.

> Acts encourages us to look for opportunities to welcome, include, and commit ourselves to others not as polite things to do but as moments of divine revelation.

When I teach Acts to seminarians, students preparing for leadership in Christian communities, I emphasize that none of these conversions occurs because someone in the church develops a strategic plan or concludes that bringing in new people will help attract more young families. In fact, no one in the church reaches out to the Samaritans, the Ethiopian, Saul, or Cornelius out of an explicit motive of remembering what Jesus said about going to certain places. The conversions take place instead because God initiates something. And the church responds. I have nothing against strategic plans for some things. My point is simply that in Acts the people of the church don't venture on their own toward new horizons of growth, reconciliation, and inclusion. The church in Acts speaks of God leading them to those places as they repeatedly discover that the good news has consequences, including the radical embrace of other people. Acts encourages us to look for opportunities to welcome, include, and commit ourselves to others not as polite things to do but as moments of divine revelation. In those moments we apprehend just how good the good news can be.

Even so, these passages remain disconcerting on several levels—and not just because they describe people having religious experiences that are very foreign to me and I suspect to many of you reading this book. What's disconcerting (but also exhilarating) is what the scenes say to Christians: expect to be changed.

Because I enjoy teaching in congregations and at gatherings of church leaders, I visit a lot of churches and I hear a lot of people say they are desperate for their church to grow or to become more diverse and inclusive. Those are good desires; they show a hunger to make sure the Christian faith remains a transformative presence in a quickly shifting society. My response is usually, "Are you yourself willing to be changed when that happens?" When people who are different from you choose to associate with "your" faith community, your job isn't to integrate them or enculturate them into the community's preexisting way of doing things. Instead the responsibility is to recognize that everyone involved is creating something new together. The scope of "you" expands. "You" will become different from who "you" were before.

Congregations that resist such change either never attract new people or lose them in a hurry. True hospitality occurs when hosts open themselves so fully to their guests that they allow the guests to transform them in the process. That kind of hospitality is on display in the Gospels, when Jesus positions himself as host and guest often at the same time, and it's a core piece of the church's experience in Acts. It indicates that a hospitable and responsive community of faith may eventually come to realize that the possibilities are endless.

Chapter 3

Discernment and Change

Passages to explore

- » Acts 6:1-6   The selection of the Seven
- » Acts 11:1-18   Peter tells the Jerusalem community about Cornelius
- » Acts 15:1-21   The council in Jerusalem
- » Acts 21:1-6   Paul in Tyre

Most people encounter the Bible in bits in pieces, such as through individual passages read aloud in worship services, chapters up for discussion at Bible studies, or snippets used to inform published prayers and devotional materials. It's an increasingly rare thing to come across Christians who have pored over entire biblical books and tried to keep track of what holds them together and how a sense of the whole contributes to one's understanding of individual passages.

That kind of big-picture outlook is vital for reading the Bible well. If we only absorb a series of passages without considering how they fit together, we are liable to miss ways in which a book tries to make its points and move its readers.

All this raises the question of what holds Acts together as a coherent whole. What is the narrative about and what drives the plot forward? It should come as little surprise that no consensus exists about exactly how to answer that question. It's not that there are no good answers; instead, there are various ways of describing the sinews that keep Acts connected into a more or less organized story. For some readers, geography is very important. They see the plot of Acts as a tale of expansion across the Roman world, beginning with Jerusalem and ending with Rome. Those readers sometimes give themselves away by flipping to the back of their study Bible to examine maps and trace Paul's journeys. For others, the stories about the two main characters, Peter and Paul, give the book a kind of dynamism. Each character becomes a little fuller and larger because of how Acts allows us to compare and contrast the two. As for me, I find it helpful to view Acts as a series of episodes propelled ahead by decisions and changes. Decision-making occurs often in Acts, and rarely are two decisions made in exactly the same way with the same kind of decision-making process. Decisions nevertheless keep the action moving.

Unless you belong to a church that has refused to change anything about its hymns, prayers, worship language, and physical space for decades or more (such places do exist!), you know that communities of believers are always making decisions about their future and the best use of their resources. Those decisions are made all the more difficult by the fact that they are *communal* decisions, requiring some kind of general agreement to go forward.

Acts is a helpful book for decision-making congregations to consider—not because it tells us exactly how to make decisions but because it understands the weight a decision can hold for Christians' common life.

Acts also complicates our decision-making, because it shows us a specific way of thinking about decisions. What happens in Acts is less about choosing and deciding and more about discerning. When I speak of discernment, I mean a process that involves reflection on who God is, what God desires, and how we—God's people—might play a part in being faithful to God's purposes. Discernment entails more than just collecting data, making projections, and choosing a sensible course of action. Discernment is an act of faith, because in the end the discerners don't say, "This is what we choose" but "This is where we think we will discover the challenges and rewards of faithfully bearing witness to Jesus." In Acts, discernment comes about as communities of believers consider their circumstances, their convictions about Jesus, their sacred texts, their lived experiences, their values, and their hopes. Not only does this advance the plot of a narrative, it also defines the church as a community always endeavoring to live into the new possibilities it believes God has in store.

Acts 6:1-6

The selection of the Seven

Every now and then I hear someone say something like this: "All of the divisions in Christianity right now make me so sad. We fight about everything. I wish we could stop all the disagreements and just be unified and harmonious, like the church originally was." Those statements misrepresent what we know about the early church, although I appreciate the desire for peacemaking that motivates them. As far back as we can look into Christian history, we see tensions, squabbles, and even outright divisions. Even in Acts, which has a tendency to soft-pedal certain disagreements that we know from other New Testament writings were more intense, occasionally tempers flare, accusations fly, and rivalries persist.

In Acts 6, no one throws rotten fruit or kicks anyone out of the church; instead, discord shows itself more subtly: through grumbling. The Greek word to describe it is *gongusmos*. It's a lovely word, because it's onomatopoeic, meaning its pronunciation sounds like what it is, like the words *buzz* and *squish*. Even "grumble" in English has the same effect. What begins as complaining in hushed voices grows louder and more disgruntled. Anyone who works with groups knows that grumbling can produce resentment and hostility, which is where especially damaging troubles live.

The cause of the grumbling appears serious. The church in Jerusalem, which has been doing an impressive job of cooperating and taking care of one another's material needs (Acts 2:44-45; 4:32-37), is having trouble with its food-distribution ministry. Maybe the church's increasing membership is straining the system. Widows are going hungry or are somehow being overlooked in the giving and receiving of charity. But not all widows. According to the accusation, Hellenist widows are victims of discrimination while Hebrew widows are not.

Acts never defines who the two groups are, but the general consensus among scholars is that in this context "Hellenists" refers to members of the church who were Greek-speaking Jews, while "Hebrews" refers to members of the church who were Hebrew- or Aramaic-speaking Jews. Linguistic and perhaps cultural divides distinguish the groups that compose what is a relatively diverse community, as we learned in our exploration of the Pentecost story in Acts 2. A logistical breakdown in food distribution would have been bad enough, but logistical problems that fall according to ethnic or cultural lines usually reveal prejudices. It's difficult to imagine another internal problem that could destroy the community as quickly as that kind of favoritism.

The apostles therefore leap into action and reorganize things, declaring that seven men with good reputations should oversee the work. The community likes the idea and chooses from its members men who all have Greek names. That doesn't necessarily mean each of them is a Hellenist, but it does suggest that the men may share affinities with that group. Apparently, the problem is solved and the grumbling ceases, for the issue never arises again.

As stories in Acts go, this one is especially unexciting. A potentially serious problem erupts, the leaders call a meeting involving the wider community to announce a solution, and the solution is implemented. No one quotes scripture, receives instruction through a vision, or calls on God to show the way. If only all of our problems were so easy to address.

Yet some aspects of the story remain troubling. At least they raise questions. Why were certain criteria set for the solution? Why didn't the explicit criteria include expertise in food distribution or intercultural sensitivity? Why were women not eligible for the job, especially the affected widows themselves? Why did the apostles assume that this kind of work was not part of their purview?

Those questions make it sound like I'm complaining that the apostles do not share my priorities or my great ideas for how their community should function. Fair enough; I wasn't in Jerusalem in the first century. And I know Acts is not a book meant for guiding believers in the fine points of organizational management. My point is that stated and unstated values always guide a church's decision-making, and there are always theological implications to the values we choose to employ. For example, balanced budgets are important, but a church's budgetary decisions can't be made solely on the basis of financial prudence or the desire to eliminate risk. Because budgets dictate priorities and direct resources in some directions and not others, budgets are also moral documents. If they're moral documents, they are theological documents, too. Every decision a church makes says something about what it understands God's desires to be, who gets to share in God's work, and exactly how a church will commit itself to the justice and reconciliation at the heart of the good news. Not every decision needs to be monumental, but no decision is purely routine.

What I appreciate most about this story is it includes no hand-wringing. When the church's ways of living begin to fail and leave the mission undone, no one puts on sackcloth and wails about the church's sin. There are times for that kind of response, but in this case the shifting membership of the church requires a new organization. Not all procedures are meant to last forever, especially if they prove discriminatory in ways that run counter to the good news. The story reminds readers that change is often a necessary consequence of congregations' successes as much as their failures.

Acts 11:1-18

Peter tells the Jerusalem community about Cornelius

In the previous chapter we explored the story of Peter and Cornelius in Acts 10, and I described it as one in a series of episodes in which God makes the implications of the good news known. The good news is for Gentiles as much as it is for Jews, because through Christ, God has done away with certain distinctions about what makes something or someone clean and what makes them polluted. As a result, Peter grows into a new understanding of the Christian community as a place where Jews and Gentiles participate together, on the same ground, in the salvation God provides.

The story does not end there, however, because not everyone reaches those conclusions as quickly as Peter does. Furthermore, the implications of Peter's new understanding apply not only to him but to the wider church as well. In fully embracing Cornelius and everyone else in his household as they are, as Gentiles who do not engage in the same dietary and purity practices Jews do, Peter does something that the rest of the church has not yet committed itself to doing. Cornelius's conversion eventually compels the wider church to reckon with whether and how it must change in response to God's initiative.

When Peter returns to Jerusalem, no one asks, "Why did you tell a Gentile about Jesus?" There's no suggestion that anyone thinks Cornelius and others are unworthy of the good news. The question—which sounds more like a rebuke—is, "Why did you go to uncircumcised men and eat with them?" Why did Peter accept hospitality from and share meals prepared by Gentiles?

Be aware that up to Cornelius's conversion every follower of Jesus in Acts is Jewish. Everyone in the church either was born Jewish or is a Gentile "proselyte," a person who converted to Judaism before embracing Jesus as the Christ. (Acts does not treat the Samaritans as non-Jews.) The only possible exception is the Ethiopian court official in Acts 8, but Acts does not follow him or his story after he and Philip separate. Acts emphasizes the Jewish identity of the church when it refers to "circumcised" people who confront Peter in this scene. The term is unfortunate in that it discounts the fact that the church was also composed of Jewish women, but nevertheless it highlights that the members of the pre-Cornelius church were concerned about more than genealogies. They were also concerned about practices dictated by Torah, the Jewish law.

Most modern Christians are so used to eating whatever we want and cleaning our homes on weekends that we've forgotten Torah observance was once the norm for most Christians in the church's earliest decades. Peter reminded God he was still keeping kosher when he saw the vision in Acts 10:14. He told Cornelius in Acts 10:28 that entering his house was not permitted. (Fun fact: nowhere in the Old Testament does it say it is "unlawful for a Jew to associate with or to visit a Gentile." That appears to be a custom that arose for a time among some—but hardly all—Jews to guard them against unwanted associations with idolatry or contamination from impure things.) No wonder the believers in Jerusalem greet Peter with such concern. Peter has acted in ways that fly in the face of generations and generations of practices that certain Jews adopted to honor God and safeguard holiness. Is he disposing of those commitments for the sake of his own convenience? Is he bringing shame to God and the church? What kind of statement is he trying to make?

Peter responds by making the longest story in Acts even longer. He and Cornelius repeated their experiences to one another in Acts 10, and now in Acts 11 Peter offers a summary appropriate for his audience. He bears witness to what happened to him, and he notes that he recognized in his new Gentile friends "the same gift" that God previously gave to him and other Jewish believers. Yet he also calls his audience's attention to something Jesus said back in

Acts 1:5: "John baptized with water, but you will be baptized with the Holy Spirit." In other words, Jesus himself authorized Peter's conclusion that God regards Gentile believers in the same light as Jewish believers, for Jesus identified the Holy Spirit as a gift from him. Peter urges his audience therefore to regard his actions as a faithful response to God's initiative, certified by Christ himself. For Peter to have acted otherwise would have been folly, an attempt to resist God.

In what looks like the most easily resolved theological disagreement in the Christian church's recorded history, the saints in Jerusalem immediately agree with Peter. They endorse his experience, his conclusions, and his behavior. No one demands that Cornelius enroll in classes on Torah observance, and no one dismisses the law of Moses as a bad thing that Jewish believers should abandon. Embedded in the verdict after the short debate is the assumption that Jewish believers and Gentile believers are going to have to get used to sharing hospitality with one another. They will need to pursue a generous unity that does not permit either group to consider itself superior to or holier than the other.

It takes a while for the perspective of the characters in this scene to take root. Similar concerns and disagreements will sprout again in Acts 15, which we will soon explore. Nevertheless, the resolution of this scene describes one of the most influential developments in the life of the early church: the conviction that Gentiles can participate fully in God's blessings through Jesus Christ without being required to abide by all the laws in Torah. If you are familiar with Paul's letters you likely know that this issue animated much of his ministry among Gentiles.

What I value most about the scene is that the means of decision-making are relatively simple and focused on the question of what kind of community God is building through Jesus Christ. No one says, "This is a great idea, welcoming Gentiles without conditions. It will really make our religion more attractive" or "I was getting tired of law observance anyway; it's time for a change." The perspective of both Peter and his discussion partners is, essentially: God has acted. The church does what it has been called to do: bear witness to Jesus and his good news with boldness and generosity. Then it watches what the Spirit does, discerns whether there's some kind of precedent for that, and follows where the Spirit leads. Discernment considers the available evidence and traditions, but then it concludes as an act of trust in God.

Acts 15:1-21

The council in Jerusalem

I apologize if you're weary of reading about Gentiles and law observance by now. Like I said, this might have been the most influential development that occurred during the church's first generation. Congregations of Jews and proselytes were part of the Christian story from the beginning, but usually everyone was expected to observe Torah, as they did before they encountered Jesus. No one appears to have anticipated that the church would become a community in which Gentiles would enjoy full inclusion without having to adopt an array of Jewish practices. That is why Acts devotes so many verses to the topic. The book is explaining a development that probably no one predicted and maybe some continued to dislike as time rolled on.

Moreover, the topic is worth our attention for reasons beyond historical curiosity. Throughout history Christians have struggled to express their religious connections with Jews as well as their distinctions from Jews in healthy, loving, and accurate ways. Exploring Acts provides some help. The narrative wants readers to know that this development was due to God's initiative and neither a marketing decision nor a severing of the church's identity as a movement initially incubated within Judaism. Acts never imagines a Gentile church coming to replace or erase its Jewish identity and origins. The history of the church's growth was much more complicated than that.

If you've ever been part of a congregation's governing body that voted on a way forward only to have someone raise the issue again a year or two later and ask to have it reconsidered, you'll appreciate Acts 15. Consequential and controversial decisions take time and patience. Discernment is difficult because so much can be at stake.

The home base for Paul—who changed his name from Saul in Acts 13—and his companion Barnabas is the church in Antioch, in Syria, whose membership consists of a considerable percentage of Gentiles. This is a different Antioch than the one in Acts 13, which we explored in the first chapter. When groups from Judea (where Jerusalem is located) tell the Antiochene Christians that their salvation is incomplete without Torah observance, Paul and Barnabas travel to settle the issue with members of the Jerusalem church.

The conference begins with Paul and Barnabas describing the vitality of their ministry among Gentiles. On the other side, some Pharisees in the church contend that law observance is necessary for all believers. Some readers may be shocked to see Pharisees belonging to the church, but that is because the term *Pharisee* has become a bad word in our contexts, facilitated by sloppy interpretations of the Gospels. The caricature is that all Pharisees were self-righteous, hypocritical, and opposed to Jesus' message of a gracious God. Everything about that description is a distortion, however, fueled by long-standing Christian animus toward Judaism. There was no reason a person could not be scrupulous about his or her own Torah observance (as the Pharisees were) and a Christian at the same time.

When Peter steps into the debate, he retells—again!—the story of his encounter with Cornelius. Notice that "God" is the subject of many verbs in his description; Peter continues to characterize the encounter as his willingness to follow God's lead. We assume the Pharisees get to make an argument, too, but Acts does not include it except to say "much debate" occurs. History is written by the winners, as they say.

James—not the apostle but one of Jesus' brothers (see Galatians 1:19; Matthew 13:55)—brings the discussion to a close. He appears to be the leader of the Jerusalem church at this point (see Acts 21:17-18). He offers a brief argument: Peter (whom he calls by his Aramaic name, Simeon) bears witness to an important truth about God's initiative among the Gentiles. Likewise, scripture (in this case, Amos 9:11-12) supports Peter's experience, for it anticipates a time when Gentiles will seek the Lord. James decides, then, that the Gentiles remain full members in the church just as they are.

James also adds a stipulation. He wants Gentile believers to avoid a few things: foods that have idolatrous associations to other gods, immoral sexual behavior (which James does not define), and eating meat that has been strangled or still has blood in it. James doesn't provide a rationale for each element of his decree, so it is difficult to explain them. One of my teachers used to quip that several Jewish writings from this period in history tend to malign Gentiles for their lack of morals by characterizing them as people who would worship anything, eat anything, and sleep with anything. In other words, James's list touches on hot topics that might have caused certain Jews to worry about indiscretions that were supposedly typical in Gentile circles: idolatry, an absence of dietary scruples, and lack of sexual restraint.

Whatever the specific reasons for James's provisions, whether his rules stem from ignorant stereotypes or legitimate concerns, they draw attention to the difficulty of maintaining unity, especially when long-standing practices and attitudes are in play. If truly God makes "no distinction" between Gentile and Jewish believers, the church will have to work hard to live out the cohesiveness that expresses that bedrock theological conviction. Eventually everyone will have to get to know and trust each other much better.

This is far from a perfect, harmonious scene. Readers have access only to certain points of view. James possesses considerable power and it isn't clear that everyone agrees. Stereotypes figure in the discussion, and no Gentile believers are on hand to speak for themselves and their own experiences. I've also never been part of a perfect discussion. There is no way of organizing a meeting or a discernment process that protects us entirely from errors or injustice. Theology—which is an abbreviation for "speaking about God"—is always messier than that, if indeed we are practicing theological discernment and not merely seeking workable solutions.

What truly amazes me is the other side should have won this debate. In other words, the advocates of law observance had centuries of tradition on their side, and that tradition was based in nuanced understandings of what it means to honor God's holiness. The only way I can make sense of how the church at large paid attention to the arguments of Acts, Paul, and others is to note that they must have believed God was doing something new. In other words, more convincing than any theological debate across a conference table were the stories of changed lives, new friendships, increased energy given to reconciliation and compassion, and unexpected experiences of solidarity and empowerment. People will follow apostles, theo-

> **They must have believed God was doing something new.**

logians, and Bible scholars only so far. It's the things that are life-giving that finally settle the debates. It's the transformative power of God's salvation that convincingly shows us where God's Spirit may be stirring.

Acts 21:1-6
Paul in Tyre

If Acts is giving you the impression that discerning God's leading is simple, clear, and something we should do casually, keep reading. It's true that often Acts proceeds with great confidence that there is one right script to follow and any Christian who's paying attention can figure it out. I know better from my own life and the stories of others. I also have experienced how manipulative and dangerous it can be when people speak carelessly about knowing "God's will" or sensing the Spirit's leading, especially when they're trying to win an argument in the process or get people to vote for their idea.

I worry about faith that loses its appreciation for wonder, mystery, and doubt, as if the Christian life is supposed to be about growing into greater certainty and control over our surroundings. I'm nourished by faith that keeps me from panicking when confronted by ambiguity and uncertainty but instead compels me to trust and be humble. I need to work on the humility part. All of that helps explain why I appreciate the short story of Paul's visit to Tyre.

Paul is on his way to Jerusalem, because he believes the Holy Spirit has prompted him to go there (Acts 19:21). He knows full well that his return to Jerusalem will mean suffering and incarceration (Acts 20:22-24) because he has accumulated powerful enemies. Yet still he goes, even though it causes distress to his friends as he travels (Acts 20:36-38; 21:12-14). He is certain that someday he will end up in Rome, and yet this is the difficult route he must follow to reach that destination.

He stops along the way in Tyre, a significant city on the edge of the Mediterranean Sea. The believers who host him urge him not to continue to Jerusalem. Although Acts doesn't make much of it or explain the Tyrians' specific reasons, it's a clash of wills. Imagine that, Christians disagreeing about the best way forward!

What's peculiar is the way Acts describes it: the believers in Tyre entreat Paul "through the Spirit." That expression is unusual, and Acts does not unpack it. (A similar expression appears also in Acts 1:2; 11:28.) It would be irresponsible, therefore, to make too much of it or to base our understanding of the Holy Spirit's influence principally on it. But it's worthwhile to ponder the expression. Do the believers of Tyre tell Paul, "For the Holy Spirit's sake, don't go!"? Or are they saying, "We believe the Spirit has told us you shouldn't go to Jerusalem"? If it's the latter, are they simply wrong? What if they're right?

Again, Acts doesn't give us enough information to answer those questions, but the short scene involves an impasse. Both sides can't be correct—that the Spirit is simultaneously leading Paul to Jerusalem while urging the Tyrians to dissuade him—or can they?

I remember wrestling with this passage in graduate school, which was the first time I ever noticed the unusual way Acts describes the Tyrians' appeal. I started grabbing commentaries to see what seasoned scholars said about the passage. I remember one, from a very respected scholar whom I won't name here, that said something to the effect of "This is a very unusual passage that underscores how difficult it is to interpret the leading of the Holy Spirit." That was all. I groaned and shut the book. I was looking for a little more wisdom from the world of biblical scholarship.

I take both parties at their word, as best as I can understand how Acts offers those words about the Spirit. Paul is convinced that the Spirit is compelling him to go to Jerusalem. The believers in Tyre appeal to the Spirit's wisdom or guidance in discouraging Paul from going. They are not standing on the same ground, and the issue is more than grief or worry. Two fundamentally different theological perspectives, each arrived at in good faith, are present.

No one panics. No one calls anyone in the other group demonic. No one leaves in a huff. In fact, Paul stays a whole week. But no one brings the other side around to their way of seeing the matter, either. Then, when they part, the scene is full of grace: all of the believers in Tyre accompany Paul and his associates to the beach, pray with him, and say goodbye as he boards a ship headed south. I'm glad they bring the children along to watch what should happen whenever Christians disagree. After the expression of unity, each group continues with their lives, presumably with a desire to be faithful in whatever is next for them.

Perhaps we never really catch up with the Spirit. What I mean is the Holy Spirit isn't to be captured, as if we somehow have access to all of the universe's secrets and can know the path to a happy and healthy life—or, in Paul's case, the path of a martyr. The goal of discernment cannot be absolute confidence or power over a situation. My reading of the rest of scripture leaves me convinced that God is more interested in the pattern of life we live than in divining some elusive specific "plan" for our individual lives. Likewise, we should be more interested in praying together with our neighbors on beaches than prevailing over them in every disagreement.

Paul and the Tyrians seem never to come to consensus about what is the right thing for Paul to do next. That doesn't mean their discernment fails. Rather, their discernment of the Spirit means they commit themselves to one another, open to the frustrations and joys of living the Christian life together as integrated parts of a larger and vulnerable body called the church.

Reflections

I'm glad Acts tells a story of believers willing to trust one another, be attentive to God, and change. I wish the narrative wouldn't make it look so easy, as if people really reach agreements so often. It's encouraging that the decision about the Gentiles' law observance takes some time to be renegotiated, but we never learn what the Pharisees and others think about the outcome. It's also encouraging to see the disagreement in Tyre, but the Tyrians enter and exit the narrative so quickly that their contributions can get overshadowed.

When I work with congregations around these passages from Acts, the stories that emerge usually confirm that discernment is difficult. What makes it challenging isn't because it endeavors to track down an invisible and evasive God, for that isn't what it's about. The difficulty lies in getting a group of believers to talk openly about who they imagine God to be. It's much easier to disagree about honoring traditions, interpreting statistics, setting priorities, and choosing which practices to adopt. When we talk about God and how we experience God's grace or the work of the Holy Spirit in our lives, most of us feel like amateurs and fear we will be exposed as pretenders. Also, that kind of talk is very intimate, for it lays bare hopes, assumptions, grievances, wounds, and joys that we might rather not share, lest others trample them or misestimate the importance they hold for us.

Acts might undersell the difficulty of discernment but it succeeds at emphasizing discernment's importance. The narrative does not promise a foolproof template for that work, nor does it promise a correct model for what church organization and leadership look like. All of that varies depending on contexts, traditions, and what works.

Take from Acts what we can observe in Acts: Christian communities, as groups called by God to live faithfully, graciously, and boldly, exist on a trajectory. That trajectory involves living into a rhythm of doing what they know to be right and beneficial to their neighbors, while always looking for ways in which God might be calling them to different or additional forms of service in a changing world. That trajectory of seeking how to live faithfully is what holds a church's larger story together.

A commitment to discernment is not a naïve fascination with newness. Christian communities should never exhibit an anxious compulsion to innovate or carelessly rewrap old reliable messages into new packaging because of fear or boredom. The church discerns because it wants to play an active role in discovering and participating in all of the experiences of community, welcome, liberation, and obedience that God has in store through Jesus Christ. Discernment proceeds from the conviction that the Holy Spirit continues to churn up those opportunities and beckon believers into them.

Chapter 4

Opposition

Passages to explore

In our explorations so far, I've been building a case for understanding Acts as a book that tells its Christian readers who they are and where they came from. It does that by heralding God's faithfulness in leading, nurturing, accompanying, correcting, comforting, and surprising the church since its beginnings. As Acts tells the story, the first generations of believers had to open themselves up to the new realities God was bringing into existence as a result of Jesus' life, execution, resurrection, ascension, and ongoing presence through the Holy Spirit. In Acts, believers do that through being obedient to Jesus' instructions, taking risks, generously loving their neighbors, and discerning together what should be a faithful response to new circumstances and opportunities.

We will find scenes that paint a clearer picture of what the church and its priorities are supposed to be, and what they are not.

Believers in Acts also make sense of who they are through conflict and hostility. The story involves growth and expansion, but also opposition and setback. Not every conflict and struggle is the same; various forces, people, and interests threaten to inhibit the people who bear witness to Jesus. Accordingly, Acts describes some conflicts differently than others and takes some more seriously than others.

Think about a few of the people or forces that have made life difficult for you. Maybe you learned to avoid or ignore some of them, just for your own sanity. Others may have caused you to fight back, seek protection, or redouble your efforts to thrive. Sometimes opposition drives us to understand ourselves better. In other words, through experiencing opposition we might clarify and recommit ourselves to who we are, what we stand for, and what we want. The result might be a sharper understanding of our identity and values.

When we explore passages about opposition in Acts, then, we are searching for more than just suspenseful stories about disagreement, strife, danger, and winners versus losers. We will find scenes that paint a clearer picture of what the church and its priorities are supposed to be, and what they are not.

Acts 1:15-20
The death of Judas

Probably the two most fascinating characters in the New Testament are Pontius Pilate and Judas Iscariot. I'm not trying to be sacrilegious. I mean that they are two people who have tremendous influence on Jesus' story and yet their states of mind or motives are difficult to determine from the four Gospels. It makes sense that preachers and thinkers have characterized them in all sorts of ways throughout history. To some, they are despicable evildoers because of their responsibility for destroying God's Anointed One. To others, they are ironic gifts from God because of the key roles they play in advancing God's intentions for the world's salvation. According to still others, they are tortured souls who deserve pity because they unwittingly do things they can't understand.

Concerning Judas, the New Testament doesn't agree. Matthew paints him as a tragic figure who kills himself because his attempts to repent go ignored (Matthew 27:3-10). Luke offers Judas no pity, for it remains silent about why he decides to turn Jesus over to the authorities except for one haunting detail: "Then Satan entered into Judas called Iscariot" (Luke 22:3). Following up on that, Jesus refers to his arrest, sufferings, and death as a manifestation of "the power of darkness" (Luke 22:53; see also 4:13). In Luke, as well as in Acts, Judas is Satan's agent.

The brief story about Judas's death in Acts 1 (which is very different from Matthew's story) includes details that illuminate his character and the nature of satanic corruption. Money and self-security figure in his downfall. Judas didn't assist those who arrested Jesus for free; it was a moneymaking venture (Luke 22:5). The bounty Judas received became the purchase price for a field. Buying land in the ancient world was one of the safest ways to hold on to large amounts of money. With the field Judas obtains a measure of security. Unfortunately for him, he does not enjoy either property or security for long. Acts suggests he falls and eviscerates himself; the land itself somehow kills him. It sounds like a grisly death. We can imagine those who first heard the story murmuring, "Just deserts."

We see more deeply into Judas's flawed character later in Acts when believers voluntarily give up their wealth—including the proceeds obtained from selling fields—as an expression of their commitment to sustain the new community of Jesus' followers (Acts 2:44-45; 4:32-37). Judas's financial decisions are nearly the opposite of the behavior that the Holy Spirit encourages within the church.

In addition, Judas's death results in a new name for the field: the "Field of Blood." At least one ancient Christian interpreter, inspired by this passage's slightly altered quotation of Psalm 69:25 and the mention of a "homestead" becoming "desolate," claimed that "Hakeldama" became contaminated with so rotten a smell that no one could stand to be there. It's like Judas ruins everything he touches.

The overdone morality of the story, especially its images of spilled entrails and a barren or defiled field, makes it resemble an etymology. Etymologies are explanations of where names come from. It's the kind of story I might have once told my children to amuse or scare them if they were to ask me in the car, "Hey, why's that field over there called Hakeldama?" There's no compassion for Judas, just as no one thinks Cruella deVil deserves a hug after the Dalmatians get away. Acts does not burden itself over Judas's fate. It would rather use him as a grotesque object lesson to define the church's values in stark contrast to what they are not.

Judas himself does not directly oppose the church in Acts. He dies before getting a chance. But the satanic influence he represents does put up a long-running fight. Judas's greed epitomizes his disregard for others' well-being and his desire to ensure his own security. Those attitudes run counter to God's salvation and thus they pollute Christian community, as we will see in other passages. The purpose of the community of believers, as declared in Acts 1:8, is to bear witness to Jesus, and that occurs in part through self-giving generosity. The church, according to Acts, in its common life embodies the liberation God provides from spiritual oppression (however we want to define that oppression). Judas is one of a few explicitly satanically tinged characters in Acts who underscore how perilous the terrain is in the ongoing quest to make that liberation a reality for all.

Acts 5:17-42

Incarceration in Jerusalem and Gamaliel's argument

For the first three chapters of Acts, nothing happens that might qualify as active opposition to the young church. That changes when Acts 4 begins and leaders of the Jerusalem Temple arrest, threaten, and eventually release the apostles Peter and John. The intimidation changes nothing, for the apostles continue their efforts as before even though the leaders order them to stop speaking in Jesus' name (Acts 4:18).

The situation grows more serious in Acts 5 when the Jewish high priest orders the apostles arrested. The incarceration is short-lived, however, because an angel liberates them and sends them back to the Temple. The angel's purpose is not to allow a clean getaway; it is to escalate the conflict. Acts relishes the outcome when it narrates the high priest and his council sitting around waiting for the prisoners to be brought only to learn that they are at that moment preaching again exactly where they were previously arrested. Not only does incarceration have no effect on the apostles, it ends up exposing the priestly authorities as powerless and foolish.

Finally, when the hearing begins, Peter and his friends are unrepentant; their responsibility to obey Jesus trumps any authority the officials can claim. This infuriates the council, and some of them wonder if assassinations or executions would settle the dispute. Suddenly a respected Torah instructor named Gamaliel stands up, sends the prisoners outside, and tries to speak sense to his colleagues.

Gamaliel reminds everyone of two popular movements centered around Jewish ringleaders. One was led by Theudas, a self-proclaimed prophet, and the other by Judas the Galilean, who was protesting new Roman tax levies. A Jewish historian who wrote around the same time Acts was composed, named Josephus, also writes about those two men, but he identifies the timing and sequence of their movements differently. Gamaliel's point is that he and his associates on the council are no strangers to revolutionary movements in the region. They don't need to risk bloodying their hands on the apostles since they can always count on the Roman military to wipe out uprisings before they grow too disruptive. Also, it's wise to hedge one's bets; waiting to see what happens is better than stumbling into resisting a movement that might turn out to be guided by God.

Gamaliel's speech and the council's approval have the air of reason, but a few details raise my eyebrows. First, even though everyone purportedly agrees, nevertheless they have the apostles beaten. That doesn't seem like the kind of thing a group of religious authorities should do if they're sincerely concerned about accidentally opposing God. Their behavior is also very disturbing to absorb during our time when we frequently find reports of extrajudicial violence in the news. Acts describes, plain and simple, a savage form of intimidation by authorities who believe they won't be held accountable. Second, Gamaliel's speech strikes me as ironic, given that readers of Acts have already learned enough to know that the apostles do indeed speak and act on God's behalf. Gamaliel's seemingly sober argument actually functions to incriminate himself and the rest of the council: they are obviously "fighting against God." They just don't know it, which makes it easier for readers to judge them harshly. They are equally violent and unperceptive—a dangerous combination.

In other words, Acts uses this occasion to characterize the council, the same body that delivered Jesus to Pontius Pilate in Luke 22:66, as opponents of both the apostles and God. Acts never reconsiders; the rest of the story carries the indictment forward. Although eventually some members of Jerusalem's priestly circle will respond positively to the good news (Acts 6:7), the same council will confront both Stephen (Acts 6:12-15; 7:54-60) and Paul (Acts 22:30–23:10) with hostility and violence. Moreover, other Jewish people in Jerusalem and beyond will oppose the church's representatives at various points in the narrative.

The depiction of so many Jewish characters as antagonistic, jealous, ferocious, and recalcitrant deserves careful attention from every Christian who reads Acts. The exaggeration is one concern, but so too is the distortion that comes whenever Acts refers casually and generally to opponents as "the Jews." I count at least thirty times in Acts when that expression is nonspecific, describing a group, a mob, or a slice of Jewish leadership. The problem is, of course, that referring to a group of opponents as "the Jews" makes it sound as though all Jews in Jerusalem or any other city are monolithically aligned against the good news. Not only is that gross hyperbole but it can draw readers away from remembering that nearly all of the protagonists in Acts are themselves Jewish. Furthermore, Jews continue to listen to the good news and respond positively up through the end of the book (Acts 28:24, 30). The story of Acts frequently involves differences of opinion *among some Jews*; it is *never* about a church that ceases to have Jewish members or about a church whose identity pits it *against* all Jews or against Judaism as a whole.

Indiscriminate references to "the Jews" in a general sense have led to disastrous consequences for the Christian church's outlook on Jews and Judaism over the centuries. If you don't know those consequences, ask a Jewish friend about them. The words of Acts remain what they are; they can't be rewritten now. But they can be reinterpreted, repentantly and responsibly. Unless we inject more nuance into our understanding of what Acts is talking about, and unless we can be honest about the ways Acts unhelpfully distorts the wide range of attitudes that Jews had toward (and within) the church during the first century, then we Christians remain complicit in ongoing sins against our Jewish neighbors.

Acts 8:9-13, 18-24
Simon the magician

Previously, when we explored the story of the Samaritans' conversion, I skipped over the verses in Acts 8 that describe one of the most notorious converts in the whole narrative: Simon the Great. Simon possesses powers that give him tremendous influence if not outright control over people's lives. Acts refers to these powers as *magic*, or wonder-working of some kind. Those wonders go beyond specific extraordinary deeds, for Acts, like other ancient writings, refers to magic in ways that criticize the motives of its practitioners. Magic was regarded as an attempt to manipulate the world's unseen forces to serve magicians' (or their clients') own purposes. Many Jews equated magic with idolatrous obedience to false gods (Deuteronomy 18:9–14). Acts is critical of magic as a lucrative practice and a reliable indicator of a person's twisted or even abusive spiritual disposition.

The cleverness of this passage's storytelling comes to light when we consider that Philip's actions—exorcisms, healings, and other wondrous acts—probably look much like Simon's. Both men exhibit "power" (using the same Greek word for each of them: *dunamis*, the source of the English words *dynamite* and *dynamic*). Yet published translations often introduce a distinction by rendering that Greek word in relation to Philip as "miracles." If Simon does something marvelous, it's "magic"; if Philip does the same kind of thing in the name of Jesus Christ, it's a "miracle."

No rivalry develops, however, for even Simon himself believes Philip's message and submits to baptism. The magician who once "amazed" the Samaritans is himself "amazed" by the works Philip performs. Simon follows him around from that point forward. From all appearances, he has been made new.

The story's outlook on Simon changes after he sees Peter and John lay hands on the Samaritan believers and they receive the Holy Spirit. He covets the apostles' apparent authority. He offers them money, which makes sense if you've learned from your whole career as a magician that a symbiotic relationship exists between money and power. You can always use one to get the other. No wonder Jesus warned his disciples about money's ability to turn people away from God (Luke 12:15-21; 14:33; 16:13).

When Peter denounces Simon, he does not criticize his basic desire to share more deeply in the church's connections to the Holy Spirit, a Spirit of *dunamis* (Luke 24:49; Acts 1:8). The problem lies in Simon's assumption that money buys a ticket to do so. Peter treats that assumption as more than just a mistake or a lesson Simon will learn in the church's new member class; it reveals Simon's ongoing captivity to wickedness. The spirit of Judas's depraved greed did not die with him in Acts 1. It lives on, manifesting itself now through Simon's unholy plan to manipulate God and ensure his own celebrity will continue.

We don't know how Simon's story ends—whether he repents or whether Peter and John's prayers make a difference for him. His time on the narrative stage ends in Acts 8:24. The open-endedness of his story, and the peculiarity of someone who believes and was baptized being revealed to have a severely corrupted heart, caught the attention of numerous Christian authors in the centuries after Acts was written. Those authors refer to Simon Magus ("Simon the Magician") as an archetype of falsehood. To them, he is the quintessential heretic: someone who knows the truth, confesses the truth, seems to submit to the truth, and yet finally reveals his authentic self when his depravity surfaces and he forfeits the truth. The exaggerated legacy of Simon Magus strikes me as unfair to the unresolved depiction of Simon in Acts 8, but that legacy illustrates an implicit aspect of the story that deserves serious attention: corruption inside a community can be as dangerous to that community as outright aggression coming from outside.

Recall that Acts is a story about, among other things, the Christian movement growing, taking root within new cultural contexts, and learning to define its identity and activity according to what God has done and continues to do in Jesus Christ. Accordingly, the challenges of the early church were about more than simply getting people's attention, adding numbers, and establishing new communities of worship and service. The challenges included learning to embody new ways of thinking and living that were guided by the good news. Following Jesus and honoring his teachings usually entail unlearning other values and patterns. As the story of Simon reminds us, some patterns that might be useful for getting ahead and staying safe in the world are poisonous to the church. Left unchecked, they erode the church's countercultural identity.

Acts 13:4-12

Bar-Jesus and Sergius Paulus

When the church expanded its existence into Samaria, Simon the Magician and his presumptions about power and manipulation created a problem. When the church expands away from the eastern edge of the Mediterranean Sea as Barnabas and Paul travel to Cyprus in Acts 13, another magician meets them there. This one also threatens to obstruct the church's growth.

Probably because I took too many Russian history courses in college, I always imagine this magician, whom Acts calls Bar-Jesus and Elymas, as looking like Rasputin, the captivating mystic, quasi-prophet, and healer who gained influence over Tsar Nicholas II during the final decade of the Romanov Dynasty. Bar-Jesus has some kind of connection to the leading Roman authority on the island, Sergius Paulus, and does what he can to prevent him from embracing the good news. I assume that Bar-Jesus fears losing his sway over the proconsul and perhaps therefore also his special access to power, wealth, and fame. People who like the way the world works for them without Jesus are often not thrilled to learn that their business associates and political partners are entertaining the prospect of following in the way of Christ.

Everything about the characterization of Bar-Jesus treats him as a villain. We've seen already that Acts considers magicians counterfeits of the true power of God experienced through the Holy Spirit. As a "false prophet" Bar-Jesus also recalls people who offer deceptions as authentic prophecies in the Old Testament as well as Jesus' disdain for false prophets (Luke 6:26). Finally, *Bar-Jesus* means "Son of Jesus," which is ironic and raises the possibility that he has been fraudulently capitalizing on Jesus' name to garner power. Before the scene ends, Paul suggests a better name would be "Son of the Devil."

Of course Paul knows something about villainy himself, although much has changed since his encounter with the Lord Jesus in Acts 9. It seems to me that Acts begs us to make connections between the two men. Both have two names in this story, for this is the turning point where Acts starts referring to Saul as Paul. (Also Paul shares a name with Sergius Paulus, adding to the fun.) The temporary blinding of Bar-Jesus recalls Paul's experience. At least in Acts 9:8 Paul had associates to guide him into Damascus. The narrative leaves Bar-Jesus behind while he's still fumbling around seeking someone to lead him by the hand. There is no promise or stated hope that he will find forgiveness. Acts treats him as simply a scoundrel whose threats to the spread of the good news need to be exposed and neutralized.

I've had students object strongly to this passage because Paul previously got a second chance for transformation and

Bar-Jesus apparently does not. Furthermore, the story celebrates the conversion of a Roman elite while a Jewish stooge gets humiliated. Also the final verse raises the possibility that Sergius Paulus believes the good news because he's impressed more by the power to disgrace Bar-Jesus than by a message of love, new life, and forgiveness.

I'm sympathetic to those students' complaints that the passage lacks compassion, and so I urge them not to build a plan for their ministry based on it alone, as if their calling is to act just like Paul does. But I also push back and urge those students to discover that the power of the story Acts tells comes in part through its delightfully stereotyped heroes and villains. Moral complexity and nuance are good things, but not every story can explore them. We don't fault the *Lord of the Rings* trilogy because no one bends over backward to make sure the nefarious wizard Saruman experiences love and forgiveness. We cheer his downfall, because he represents the horrors that erupt when corruption, betrayal, and cowardice gain access to power. We need to recognize what kind of story Acts is trying to tell and why it sometimes speaks in such one-sided ways. Once we do that, then we can move on to account for life's complexities.

The satanic energy and influence we previously witnessed in Judas are present also in Bar-Jesus. It's subtle, but Paul's reference to him as "Son of the Devil" supports the idea that a satanic shadow lies behind Bar-Jesus' opposition. That opposition expresses itself in greed, lust for power, and a desire to ensure one's own security by any means necessary (see also Acts 5:3). As Acts sees it, there is no negotiating with the satanic grip on this world; God intends instead to defeat it and free the world from it.

Acts 25:1-12
Paul appears before Festus

The Roman Empire puts up opposition in Acts. It also opens up opportunities.

It's too abstract to talk about "the empire" in general terms. I am talking in particular about Roman officials and their responsibility to protect Roman economic, social, and political interests. We briefly met one of those officials, Sergius Paulus, on Cyprus in Acts 13. He was not in the narrative spotlight long enough to do much to advance or deter the movement of the word of God, although he did believe what he learned from Barnabas and Paul. Additional local officials show up briefly and respond positively, such as Dionysius the Areopagite (Acts 17:34) and Publius of Malta (Acts 28:7). It's a different story with others, some of whom we will spend time with later, in chapter 6. The ones who present the greatest challenges are those we meet in Acts 21–26.

Over the final quarter of the narrative, from Acts 21:33 to the final verse, Paul is in Roman custody. More than four years elapse, and during most of that period he remains largely quarantined from ordinary society. While incarcerated he is able to interact, however, with high-ranking Roman officials, mostly men Acts calls "governors," the chief officials over the province. The story moves slowly compared to the rest of Acts. There are hearings, speeches, transfers, and even a sea voyage with a shipwreck to spice things up.

Paul finds himself in custody not because he has committed an obvious crime but because a group of Jews in Jerusalem, including the high priest and the chief priests, want him dead. Various Roman officials keep him incarcerated for several reasons. They want to protect him because they aren't sure he deserves to die and they suspect that releasing such a divisive figure will, whether his enemies end his life or not, trigger unrest among Jews in Judea. They are compelled to protect his legal rights even though they suspect it might be advantageous for everyone involved—at least, everyone who has a share in Roman privilege and political power in the region—if someone killed him. They find it easier simply to hold on to him while time elapses and increases the chances his enemies will calm down, his friends will pay a bribe for his freedom, or some other official will finally figure out what to do with him.

On one hand, then, Paul is stuck in political gridlock. On the other hand, he now has access to very influential figures, and so he uses this occasion to tell them about Jesus, when they will listen. As Acts tells Paul's story, it's an interesting paradox. All the political, legal, and military muscle in the region purports to control and restrict Paul, and yet he finds opportunities to preach the good news to new audiences of people who would ordinarily be inaccessible to him. The Roman governors and their underlings are the opposition. They also are the opportunities. It's one of the ways in which Acts declares God to be more powerful and more worthy of praise than any leader or aspect of the Roman Empire.

In Acts 25, Paul has been held in Caesarea Maritima, where the governor's primary residence was, for two years. A newly appointed governor, named Porcius Festus, has not spent time with Paul but quickly surmises that this prisoner gives him a valuable bargaining chip in his ability to win favor with the priestly aristocracy. Festus needs the priests on his side, for they hold responsibility for keeping peace in the region so the Roman imperial machine can operate as intended. Unnecessarily exacerbating the tensions between the governor and the Jewish elites in Jerusalem could be a quick way for any imperial appointee to be removed from office. It had happened before.

Paul detects a ruse. This isn't the first time a group has planned to ambush him (Acts 23:12-24). He refuses to surrender his life to sweeten the music for the political dance between a Roman governor and the Temple leaders. He demands a transfer to Rome so he can plead his case before the emperor himself. Paul is tired of playing games; it's time for him to bring what he has to say to the man at the top of the imperial hierarchy. Festus grants the request, which sets the stage for two major developments: Paul gains an opportunity to defend himself and his faith in Christ before Festus, King Herod Agrippa II and Bernice, and the highest ranking men of Caesarea (Acts 25:13–26:32); and Paul is able to go to Rome, which is where he has been planning to end up since Acts 19:21.

Some people conclude that Acts portrays Paul as an innocent man who simply tries to get a fair hearing. His ability to navigate through the morass of Roman justice encourages readers to live blamelessly even in difficult times. I disagree. The emphasis lies elsewhere. I think Acts is not very interested in settling the question of Paul's guilt or innocence according to the outlook of Roman law and privilege. Acts is more determined to show readers that the obstacles Roman authorities put in front of the message about the good news are finally not as menacing as they appear at first glance. Paul somehow manages to leverage his legal proceedings. No one can control him or his message.

That isn't to say that Acts wants everyone to revel in Paul's cleverness and survival instincts. Instead, through Paul's extended custody Acts makes statements about the Roman Empire. Even one of the most formidable political and cultural forces ever to appear in history can be subverted or hijacked, in a way, for God's intentions to become realized. It only looks like Rome makes the rules and controls lives. Paul and the readers of the narrative understand that the glories of Roman power are really illusions. In indirect defiance Acts says, to God be the glory.

> Even one of the most formidable political and cultural forces ever to appear in history can be subverted or hijacked, in a way, for God's intentions to become realized.

Reflections

I'm not going to conclude this exploration of opposition by asking you to name the church's enemies today. I'm not interested in encouraging even more people to treat the Bible as a tool for drawing thicker lines between groups, as if scripture somehow urges us to assign everyone in the world to a particular category. Nor do I want to equate all "opposition" with "enemies." Based on the passages we've explored, I believe a more appropriate question than "Who is the enemy?" is "How should believers respond faithfully and responsibly to whatever impedes their ability to live out the generosity and hospitality of the good news?"

I find it remarkable that Acts does not worry much about the people and forces that threaten the vitality of Christian ministry from the outside. Yes, Paul has his adversaries and the Roman desire to safeguard the status quo is formidable, but the witness of the church continues nevertheless. Acts has every confidence that the promise of new life in Christ is more powerful than any potential opposition. Setbacks may come, and the story includes violence and loss, yet Acts never expresses doubt about the eventual outcome. The word of God will continue to persevere.

It's also noteworthy that Acts depicts certain attitudes and values as toxic to the church. As someone who spends a lot of time in churches and observes their frailty (because it doesn't take many bad actors to ruin a congregation), I appreciate that Acts warns about the corrosive potential of greed and power. Divisive people are no help, either (Acts 20:28-30).

I've commented on the necessity of working carefully with how Acts speaks of "the Jews" and especially the characters in the narrative who pursue violence or legal action against members of the church. The issue deserves a little more attention. Remember that Acts is up to more than recounting stories for the sake of remembering history. The writing of Acts is a piece of a larger, complex period in time when the Christian church was working out its own identity. Part of that involved distinguishing the church *from* certain Jewish groups. Acts carries the pain of disagreements that occurred *within* ancient Jewish communities that were once connected but eventually divided in their response to the good news. Acts also reflects hostility that emerged once the church became virtually *separate from* many Jewish communities. That pain and hostility can be acknowledged without being replicated by us as readers of Acts today. I urge preachers and Bible readers all the time to beware of caricatures and historical inaccuracies they may have inherited. When it comes to reading Acts and its frequent references to "the Jews," be sure to look at the context of each reference and ask: exactly which Jewish people is Acts talking about? Specific leaders? A limited group? The general population of a particular town?

Finally, I confess I get uneasy with Christians who place too much focus on satanic power. I'll have to write another book to explain the details. Acts doesn't talk much about the devil, but it does describe the good news as able to turn people "from the power of Satan to God" (Acts 26:18). I see plenty of wickedness in our individual choices, our corporate existence, and the systems and policies we have constructed to govern how we allot opportunities to some people but not others. Attributing all that to "Satan" sounds too convenient and hasty to overlook the evil that humanity generates all on its own. At the same time, Acts contends there is a persistent sickness about the world and the status quo that only God can overcome. Through Jesus Christ God accomplishes a liberation we cannot achieve by ourselves.

Fortunately Acts includes many sketches of what liberated life looks like, even as opposition and evil remain ever present. As we will soon see, in Acts there are inspiring examples of people embodying that kind of life all around.

Chapter 5

Saints around the Edges

Passages to explore

Whoever it was—not the author, but someone in later generations—who first coined the title *The Acts of the Apostles* made a big mistake. It's not a helpful title, because the book tells us very little about the apostles. Roughly the first half of Acts tells stories about Peter, leaving us largely in the dark about other members of "the Twelve," such as Bartholomew and my favorite apostle, Matthew. We know that Judas dies and Matthias replaces him in Acts 1, but what are the rest of Jesus' chosen apostles up to? Stephen and Philip also spend a little time in the narrative spotlight in Acts 6–8, but Acts doesn't consider them apostles, technically speaking. Paul is the predominant character throughout the second half of the book. At first glance, then, the book is *The Acts of Peter and Paul*. It looks like a narrative about two heroic individuals who were essential for the growth and survival of the young church.

That is not the whole story, though. From other writings in the New Testament, we know that the early Christian movement included many noteworthy and influential men and women, not just Peter and Paul. Obviously, Acts is not trying to tell "the history of the early Christian church," if we understand that to mean that Acts is telling *the* one complete or comprehensive history, or that we can speak of *the* early church as a single, totally coordinated organization.

The author of Acts plainly knew that there were more stories that could have been told, that the churches that came into being during the three decades after Jesus' death and resurrection were composed of believers who had various gifts and numerous ways of being influential. The early church consisted of much more than a handful of charismatic leaders who seemed to know the right things to say in every circumstance or who slyly and maybe miraculously managed to avoid death longer than one might have expected. We can find traces of some of those additional believers in Acts.

The people who operate at the fringes of the plot may not receive as much attention as Peter and Paul, but they are equally important to our understanding of what the first generations of believers did to help build the new society that God's Spirit was creating among them. They help us understand, first, the *history* of the church better. We know and need to celebrate that in the first century all sorts of people played parts in leading the church in both public and out-of-the way settings. Second, they help us understand the *theology* of the church better. Acts attests that God is present among communities of believers and the work they do. God calls everyone to live out his or her faithfulness in whatever ways might bear witness to Jesus. God is active when people contribute to communities in which people care for one another, share their resources, learn, and worship. If we make Peter's and Paul's actions the standard, we're bound to overlook countless other opportunities to serve and encounter God in our own lives.

I'm not interested in being part of a church that builds its notion of leadership only around the highly visible, valiant, and nearly daredevil portraits of Peter and Paul. I've discovered the renewing power of the Holy Spirit in other settings and among other kinds of people. I think Acts acknowledges this, too.

Once we shine a light into certain parts of the book, we discover that some of the influential saints are women. They remind us that public leadership in the early church was not exclusively a boys' club. Some of those saints are dislocated people. They remind us that spiritual discovery often comes from putting ourselves in close contact with people different from ourselves. Some saints appear to have lacked the means and social capital to travel beyond where they lived. They remind us that the church does not operate with conventional criteria for what counts as an influential contribution to our shared life. Some suffered, reminding us that Christian discipleship involves sharing in Jesus' own experiences. Some were willing to stand up and push back when they disagreed with other leaders. They remind us that no single person has exclusive claim to discerning the leading of the Holy Spirit or defining every aspect of the good news.

Acts 1:12-14

The 120 people in an upper room

My favorite chapters in the New Testament are Luke 1–2. There, faithful people such as Elizabeth, Zechariah, Mary, Simeon, and Anna react to the births of John the Baptist and Jesus as indications that God is at last fulfilling old promises. Those characters foresee grand things to come and believe a new page in the world's history is turning. They have special insight into what is going on. They give voice to what they perceive. They wait faithfully for what God will accomplish. Their testimonies and worship urge us to expect big things as the gospel story gets underway.

Something similar happens in Acts 1, immediately after Jesus promises the Holy Spirit will come and then ascends to Heaven. The apostles gather in Jerusalem, waiting for the Spirit, and we read that they "were constantly devoting themselves to prayer, together with certain women, including Mary the mother of Jesus, as well as his brothers." In the following verse (Acts 1:15), we learn that the full company of believers in Jerusalem was around 120 people. This is the group who will speak about God's good news in Acts 2, once Pentecost arrives.

The group consists of more than apostles. Presumably many of them are part of "the whole multitude" (Luke 19:37) who accompanied Jesus when he entered Jerusalem several weeks earlier. We can reasonably assume that Mary Magdalene, Joanna, Susanna, and the numerous additional women who followed Jesus throughout his public ministry (Luke 8:1-3; 23:55) were also part of the group. Mary is definitely there, a key part of the unfolding action just as she was in Luke 1. Together all of them wait for what God will do next, which is evidence of their trust and commitment.

> Christians can look at insurmountable challenges and believe God will not abandon them. Death is not the last word. God's encouragement manifests itself in places and people where most observers see only hopelessness.

Acts does not comment on their state of mind, but I would be praying my heart out, too, if I were in their sandals. Excitement, high hopes, and terror must have permeated their gatherings. Less than two months earlier their friend and leader was executed in the same city as an enemy of the Roman Empire. They saw him resurrected. He told them that work awaits them as his "witnesses" in the world. The grandiose promises of salvation and restoration articulated by the saints in Luke 1–2 have not yet completely come to pass. But the connections drawn between the beginning of Acts and the Gospel of Luke, such as the presence of the same characters in both books, signal that the promises are still valid. God is bringing something new into being.

From my perspective, one of the most compelling and motivating aspects of Christian faith is its ability to perceive reality differently. Christians can look at insurmountable challenges and believe God will not abandon them. Death is not the last word. God's encouragement manifests itself in places and people where most observers see only hopelessness. Evil and injustice can be thwarted by love. Do those 120 people believe all of that? It isn't clear that they've fully arrived yet. But there they are, waiting as an act of faith and obedience.

Acts 2:43-47

The generous community formed at Pentecost

If you recall our previous exploration of the Pentecost story in Acts 2, you probably remember the visible and audible manifestations of the Holy Spirit, the crowds, the many languages, and Peter's sermon to the masses. There's one more piece to Pentecost, however: the Holy Spirit calls a new community into existence.

Acts 2 concludes with the creation of a community characterized by fellowship, worship, unity, and charity. Community—the collection of ordinary people going about everyday life but with an extraordinary commitment to one another—shows up all over Acts. When people respond to the good news, Acts almost always mentions in the same breath a larger fellowship or an occasion of hospitality. The narrative emphasizes that Peter and Paul work with others and maintain close connections with communities of faith. Salvation, according to Acts, isn't individualistic. It involves belonging to and participating in a larger, expansive community.

When I teach in churches about this passage and a similar one in Acts 4:32-37, someone invariably asks, "Was that real?

Did all of that sharing really happen?" Those questions don't always arise when we read stories about a sick person being healed or someone hearing directly from God in a vision. Maybe it's easier for some of us to accept stories about miracles than one about Christians taking care of one another in such self-giving and harmonious ways. The way of life in the nascent Jerusalem church seems too good to be true, or we worry that it makes us look bad today.

Whether things were actually once as fabulous as Acts suggests or not, the truly amazing thing to consider is that somehow the fledgling church survived during its earliest days in Jerusalem. Lots of Jesus' followers, adults who knew how to make a living farming and fishing in rural Galilee, would have needed help surviving in the crowded and land-locked city. The same is true for other travelers who found their way into this community because of Pentecost. To keep everyone there, people would have had to have shared money and hospitality. Tables had to be open to newcomers. Acts talks a lot about people preaching, explaining, and arguing. But behind all of that activity is a group of people who are so convinced that God is doing something new that they commit themselves to new ways of living. Together.

Acts 6:8-15; 7:54-60
The death of Stephen

Stephen is hardly a character "around the edges" in Acts. He gives the longest speech in the whole book and goes down in church tradition as the first "martyr"—someone killed as a result of his or her faith in Jesus Christ. Stephen deserves our attention because his story is so different from many other characters' in Acts and yet he establishes a pattern for what all disciples can expect.

Christians, Acts declares, can expect to follow in Jesus' footsteps. That's true with the public ministry Stephen performs "among the people," and it also is written into the story of his death. Stephen faces false testimony against him, with people accusing him of being anti-Temple and anti-law as he stands before the highest religious authorities in Jerusalem. After Stephen's long speech fails to convince anyone, the details of his brutal execution recall Jesus' own experience. Like Jesus in Luke 23:46, Stephen dies while expressing confidence in God. Stephen prays for his killers' forgiveness, as Jesus did in Luke 23:34.

People sometimes deride Acts as a book that promulgates a "theology of glory," in which the church's successes and survival take center stage while setbacks and suffering are conveniently omitted. Stephen might beg to differ with that assessment. Just as Jesus' activity continues in the life of the early church, so too does Jesus' rejection. No one said being his witnesses would be easy.

So many scenes in Acts involve conflict or potential for conflict. All kinds of believers get caught up in it. Along the way, Acts might occasionally be guilty of portraying the villains of the story as a little too villainous, to the point of unhelpfully caricaturing the church's opponents. The main storyline of Acts nevertheless retains a valid point: something about the good news that the church declares and embodies is capable of turning the world upside down (Acts 17:6). Usually the people who lead and benefit from the world as it is currently organized resist that kind of turning.

Acts 9:36-43

The ministry and raising of Tabitha/Dorcas

From one perspective, this story celebrates Peter and his ability—rather, God's ability working through Peter—

to raise a dead person back to life. That's too limited a perspective, however, because the dead person is more than just an ordinary corpse to reanimate. She's Tabitha. She's also Dorcas. She's a person. She has two names. She has a life-giving ministry.

Healing stories in the Gospels and Acts rarely pause to tell us much about the person being healed; instead, they go straight to the action. This episode is different. We learn the person's name, and Acts describes how important she was to the community she left behind at her death.

Her name is "Gazelle," because that's what both *Tabitha* (Aramaic) and *Dorcas* (Greek) mean. By referring to her with both names, Acts insinuates that she lives in a multilingual environment. Perhaps she has friends who speak Aramaic and others who speak Greek. Imagine a pastor today who is called Lucía by some and Lucy by others as she greets familiar people while shopping in the local grocery store. The woman who is returned to life in Acts 9 sounds like a bridge builder in her community. This would have made her an especially valuable person as the Christian movement was spreading and incorporating different kinds of Jews from different locations and backgrounds into a new fellowship.

We also learn that a group of widows mourns her passing. Not all widows in the first century were poor and vulnerable, but some were. In any case, the Bible often treats widows as women who face jeopardy in their male-dominated society and economy. That seems to be the case in this scene, as the widows have received precious gifts from Tabitha/Dorcas: clothing. What an intimate and caring gift. Making clothes for someone else requires you to know that person—what size she wears, what she likes, what you think is appropriate for her needs and personality. The tenderness of the brief encounter between Peter and the grieving widows is about more than infusing the scene with pathos. It's to make us aware of the substantial ministry that Tabitha/Dorcas performed among the believers in Joppa. She helped knit the community together, literally clothing the people with protection, beauty, dignity, and love.

No wonder Acts refers to her as a "disciple" and a woman "devoted to good works and acts of charity." Peter doesn't bring her back to life as a reward for her good behavior or because he can't handle all the tears being shed. Bringing her back to life validates the urgency of her work. This doesn't mean she herself doesn't matter; of course she does. But we assume Tabitha/Dorcas will not live forever. Eventually death will overtake her a second time, after her story in Acts ends. But the leadership and material sustenance she provides now has an opportunity to live again—through her ongoing efforts and the charity that is supposed to dwell at the center of every Christian community. She may not enjoy the same adventures that Peter has in Acts, but this passage insists her contributions are just as essential to the church's ability to bear witness to the wholeness Jesus Christ brings to individuals and communities.

Acts 11:19-26
The ministry of Barnabas

We first meet Barnabas in Acts 4:36-37, when he offers the proceeds from a land sale to support the believers in Jerusalem. He appears again in Acts 9:26-27, when he vouches for Saul because everyone else remains unconvinced that the former persecutor has really given up his violent ways.

Clearly Barnabas enjoyed a good reputation among the church in Jerusalem. Acts portrays him as a risk taker who is committed to helping others. Someone even once thought he deserved the nickname *Son of Encouragement*, although it isn't clear how that name might have connected to *Barnabas* (which itself is a nickname, given that the man's original name was Joseph). *Barnabas* does not translate into "Son of Encouragement" in either Aramaic or Hebrew.

It's his character that mattered, anyway, and not the origins of his names. No wonder the Jerusalem church sends him to Antioch to assist the new and fast-growing church there. Surely someone realized that he would be invaluable to the attempts to keep the different kinds of believers— both Jews and Gentiles (for the word *Hellenists* in this context refers to non-Jews)—unified in their new existence as Christians.

Barnabas also sees an opportunity to get Saul involved, even though no one asked him to do so. He's still working to help the church's former archenemy live into what Jesus has planned for him. Barnabas appears to believe more than anyone else that God will use Saul to bring the good news to many. Without Barnabas, Saul might have stayed in Tarsus.

Barnabas sees the gifts that someone else possesses and makes sure they get used. His encouragement and friendship lay the groundwork for ministry to continue and to expand. People like him always change the church's story.

Acts 12:1-17
The insight of Rhoda

Just before King Herod Agrippa I, a client king ruling on behalf of Rome, completes his plan to execute Peter, who is incarcerated and under heavy guard, the apostle *par excellence* gets away. Good thing the church was praying so fervently for him. This scene is the second of three occasions in Acts when God makes it possible for a prominent evangelist to escape incarceration. The narrative is fond of showing that imperial muscle is no match for God's power. (Although Acts doesn't presume that God's power is always ready to save the day. Remember, the apostle James falls victim to Herod's violence at the beginning of Acts 12.)

Peter's journey from custody to freedom is so amazing that even he thinks it's all a hallucination until he finds himself alone and outside the city's formidable iron gate. What will he do next? He's out of his chains but hardly out of danger. God delivers him only so far. God doesn't open each and every door to freedom. Now Peter needs to finish the job. So he goes to his friends, where he can be safe.

He travels to the home of a woman named Mary. You're forgiven if you find it confusing that there are so many women named Mary in the New Testament. It was a popular name among Jews in that region. This one, the mother of John Mark, appears nowhere else in the Bible. Mary's home has a gate outside it, but it does not open as easily for Peter as the large gate that secures the city. The believers gathered inside to pray don't see a good reason for opening it. They're so busy praying for Peter that they don't expend any effort to learn whether their prayers have actually made a difference.

Good thing Rhoda is in the house. She is a young slave (not a "maid"), and she recognizes Peter's voice. She's the only one with the ability to imagine that a prayer has been heard. Unfortunately no one listens to her.

Peter can't believe that God is liberating him until his escape is over and he somehow comes to his senses. His friends gathered in Mary's home can't believe that their prayers for his life could have changed anything. But Rhoda believes.

Rhoda's story reminds us not to idealize the early church. We can't assume that Acts always depicts Christians having great insights, making the right choice, and living upstanding lives. Rhoda is made to live as a slave in a Christian home, for one thing. No one in Acts sees a problem with that! And she's dismissed as delusional when she reports the truth. Rhoda's experience resembles the moment in Luke 24:11, when the women who found Jesus' tomb empty were dismissed and discredited by the rest of Jesus' followers. I suspect it's difficult for people to accept a message of good news when they harbor disdain toward the messenger.

I have a friend, also a New Testament scholar, who dislikes the narrative's portrait of Rhoda. To her, Rhoda is treated as a comedic figure, which allows readers to disrespect any wisdom she possesses. The scene's silliness also lessens the offense we might experience toward that fact that *she is a slave owned by a family of believers*. Like the foolish Prissy in *Gone with the Wind*, Rhoda is difficult to take seriously, because of how Acts presents her. My friend has a point, in that Acts makes it much too easy for readers to dismiss Rhoda both as a fool who fails by leaving Peter outside and as someone who deserves her circumstances because she appears not smart enough to make it through life on her own. But still I think Rhoda stands out for this: she takes herself seriously. She takes her testimony seriously. She knows what she has seen and heard, and she won't waver in declaring it until everyone else finally comes to know what she knows. In that small detail, she shows herself more willing to discover the power of prayer than anyone else.

The church keeps Rhoda as a slave, but that can't keep her insight from roaming free. She sees that God is bringing a story of deliverance to a good ending, even when everyone else's lack of trust tries to keep her and her hope confined.

Acts 13:1-3

The diverse set of believers in Antioch

Saul and Barnabas have been absent from the narrative stage for a little while until the very end of Acts 12 arrives. During that time they were part of the thriving Christian community in Antioch in Syria (Acts 11:19-26). With the beginning of Acts 13, however, they are launched into a new chapter of ministry. Their journey will take them far away and be a milestone in the larger story of the good news finding traction within a wide range of settings and cultures. But Barnabas and Saul don't go alone or entirely of their own will. Representatives of the wider church send them out, believing the Holy Spirit has called them to commission a new venture into the church's future.

It's a short story, but Acts identifies three main characters who are among the leaders of the Antiochene church: Simeon who was called Niger, Lucius of Cyrene, and Manaen. These men are mentioned nowhere else in the New Testament, unless Paul's passing reference to a Lucius in Romans 16:21 refers to the same person. Who are they?

From the few words Acts uses to identify these prophets and teachers, we can see that the church retains its Pentecost diversity. The First Christian Church of Antioch is multicultural, composed of people whom God has brought together from different backgrounds. The small group mentioned here has a cosmopolitan character; it represents a relatively wide extent of physical and social geography.

Simeon is principally a Jewish name, and his other name, *Niger*, is the Latin word for "black." We don't know for certain the story behind the second name, which could be a nickname. It would not be far-fetched if it was a reference to his skin color. In the first century there were

Jewish communities in Africa, both Northern Africa and sub-Saharan Africa, just as there still are today. Simeon or his ancestors may have come from one of those places.

Lucius was a common name derived from Latin, and this Lucius was clearly African, for he had origins in Cyrene, which was located in what is now Libya. There was a well-established Jewish community in Cyrene at that time. Like anyone else in Antioch, Lucius could have been Jewish or Gentile.

Manaen's name is the Greek equivalent of the Hebrew *Menachem*. He had some kind of connection to Herod Antipas, the son of Herod the Great who ruled Galilee and nearby lands during Jesus' lifetime. The expression describing the specific connection between the two men is ambiguous. Manaen might have once been a government official (a "member of the court") or he might have been the ruler's "childhood friend." Either way, in his past and maybe still in his present he rubbed shoulders with his society's most elite and influential members.

If you were present when the church gathered for worship in Antioch, you would have seen different skin colors and different styles of clothing. You would have heard different accents and perhaps multiple languages. You would have heard teachers telling stories about their experiences of God's faithfulness in different kinds of cultural settings and within different kinds of family systems and inherited traditions.

I imagine that's part of the reason why in these verses everyone seems so confident about the need to send Saul and Barnabas away. This appears to be a community of believers that has taught itself how to listen. I would wager it's by listening well to one another, appreciating the differences among them, that they learned how to hear God's Spirit.

When Saul and Barnabas set sail for Cyprus and beyond, the church stands on the cusp of growing much larger, in terms of its geographical extension. It will also receive all sorts of new members, welcoming all the wonders and challenges of increased diversity in the process. The saints in Antioch, who possess widespread cultural wisdom, do their part to prepare their church and their missionaries to be that kind of community.

Acts 18:1-4, 24-28
The ministry of Priscilla, Aquila, and Apollos

Aquila and Priscilla were a power couple in the early church. We learn about them in Acts and also in some of Paul's letters. They were traveling missionaries, teachers, and hosts of a house church (1 Corinthians 16:19). They found themselves expelled for a time from Rome because of an edict from Emperor Claudius that applied to Aquila and possibly also to Priscilla. Yet they also eventually found themselves in Paul's company in Corinth. All three of them were leatherworkers. All of them possessed the financial means and social expertise to be mobile. All of them were eager to spread the good news about Jesus.

When Paul leaves Priscilla and Aquila in the large city of Ephesus, several changes occur. First, the narrative turns to describe action unrelated to Paul for a few verses, which is rare in the second half of Acts. Second, Acts begins referring to the couple with Priscilla's name first. This is subtle, but it probably indicates either that she was the more prominent or gifted of the two or that she occupied a higher social stratum than her husband. In either case, she is hardly an ornament to Aquila. Third, the wife-and-husband team plays a key role in graciously guiding a charismatic teacher named Apollos toward a more accurate understanding of the good news. If Priscilla and Aquila were inclined to be a little more combative, they might have chosen instead to denounce him publicly. But what good would that have done?

Just a few verses contain so many experiences that influence so many

The first generations of Christians had no instruction manuals. They were constantly required to answer the question, *What does it look like to live out our faith in this particular time and place?*

lives. In Ephesus, on the western edge of modern Turkey, a married couple exiled from Rome encourage and gently correct the teachings of an energetic young minister from Alexandria (northern Egypt) so he might be more effective when he goes to Achaia (western Greece).

I often remind myself that the first generations of Christians had no instruction manuals. They were constantly required to answer the question, *What does it look like to live out our faith in this particular time and place?* Disagreements were frequent. Other teachers with different ideas might have appeared threatening. The pressure for believers to conform to social norms—knowing when to stay in one's lane concerning matters of economic status, gender, family, and age—must have been intense. A passage like this one suggests, albeit simply, that some Christian communities made their way through those challenges by committing themselves to one another, by finding a place in their midst for refugees, by honoring one another's God-given gifts, and by building on the things that connected them as opposed to exacerbating the factors that might keep them apart.

Reflections

If you belong to a faith community, how do you and the rest of the congregation tell the story of who you are and where you came from? Do you list membership figures, names of pastors, and significant stages in developing your real estate through the years? Or do you talk about the ways in which the church and surrounding neighborhood have interacted over time, in terms of demographics, programs offered, and the consequences of changes in the local economy? Or do you talk about what exactly has spurred you to learn who you are and what you are to do—how God has faithfully shaped your identity through good times and bad, and how certain people and their work have inspired resilience or helped the congregation imagine new ways forward?

All of those kinds of historical storytelling have value, but the third way is the most revealing. It usually calls attention to the Holy Spirit's ability to shape a community's ethos and identity either subtly over time or urgently in the fray of a crisis. It likewise calls attention to the severe damage that occurs when a community succumbs to toxic ways of living and other bad influences.

Acts was written to remind churches at the end of the first century that they stood in the legacy of God's faithfulness to the first generations of Christians. Acts wasn't pining to return to the past, as if to say, "I wish Peter and Paul were still alive; they'd know what we have to do next." Acts was declaring that the word of God could still be heard, as it always has been, in the corporate existence of the church. God's salvation manifests itself in the ways ordinary people once bore witness to the power of the good news, and how that power still brings people into nurturing communities, exposes and heals injustices, and creates new friendships that are not restricted by old lines of separation. As a result of that power, the people of God experience newfound wholeness and boldness through worship, learn to walk in the forgiveness available for the evils they have committed and suffered, encounter God in times of suffering, and do their part to nudge the world toward alignment with God's intentions for humanity's well-being.

Granted, Acts tells its story by focusing on the public work of a small number of influential men, accentuating the controversial and disruptive aspects of the early church's outward-facing recruitment efforts. The book's overriding focus on Peter and Paul, especially on their public speaking skills and dogged survival instincts, has contributed to problems through the centuries. It has been used by those who persistently cling to the lie that only men are suited to hold certain religious offices. It has tempted the church to embrace the ideals of celebrity culture in its ways of measuring the effectiveness of its leaders and ministries. It has diminished our ability to value and honor the gifts and insights of people among us, especially the gifts that keep people fed, clothed, and safe. It may also have supported congregations' tendencies to be safe havens for bigotry, allowing us to forget the diversity and varied experiences that have always been a part of God's desires for the church.

That is why I urge anyone who reads Acts to commit to poke around in the narrative, searching for evidence for how this book imagines the church living as a new society, inhabited and led by many kinds of disciples. Some of those saints might dwell at the edges of the story Acts tells, but they're at the center of any church's vitality. The more we're able to locate and celebrate those saints within Acts, the better we'll be able to discern God's faithfulness around us. We'll discover that same faithfulness in the testimonies and efforts of the believers living and working in our orbit. And each of us will know the value of our own stories and actions as well.

Chapter 6

This Changes Everything

Passages to explore

- » Acts 14:8-20   Confusion in Lystra
- » Acts 16:11-40   Hostility in Philippi
- » Acts 17:1-9   Uproar in Thessalonica
- » Acts 19:11-41   Resistance in Ephesus

According to the Gospels, Jesus spoke about "the kingdom of God" more than any other topic. He wasn't talking about a place, like a far-off heaven where none of our problems can follow us. "The kingdom of God" refers to the state of affairs in which God's gracious intentions for humanity and all creation finally become fully actualized. That new reality begins to emerge in Jesus' presence and activity, here on earth (Luke 17:21). That's good news.

People who say that Jesus wasn't interested in politics

misunderstand that at the heart of his message and his compassionate deeds was a vision for a new society—a different way for people to live together into the wholeness, justice, human flourishing, reconciliation, and generosity that God desires. Anyone who talks about making that kind of existence a reality is unavoidably stepping into political currents, because all of those topics have implications for how people organize their communities, what values will characterize their life together, who gets to possess power over others, and whose needs will have priority. The chief political authority over Jesus' region understood. Pontius Pilate had reasons for his severe response to Jesus. Torturing him, choosing to execute him publicly by crucifixion, and hanging a sign reading "King of the Jews" on the cross were all political statements about the superiority of Rome's privileges and values if there ever were any. From Rome's perspective, Jesus and his vision deserved to be humiliated and exterminated.

I don't want to draw overly simple connections between our "politics" today and the political character of the kingdom of God that Jesus announced and enacted. My point is to note that Jesus' life was taken from him because powerful people benefited from the status quo and the social, political, economic, and religious systems in place to preserve it. His death was no accident. It was a calculated response to a perceived threat. It wasn't simply that powerful people didn't like Jesus. They didn't like the values and social ideals for which "the King of the Jews" was advocating.

Threats to "business as usual" in the Roman-controlled world continue in Acts. Jesus' followers bear witness to their leader, a man executed as an enemy of the state and raised again to demonstrate God's power over death. Even if Acts rarely portrays the church's representatives as deliberate agitators, nevertheless the kingdom of God that they preach and embody has a way of challenging the status quo and its prevalent values. Their conception of God and the

> A commitment to Jesus affects everything about a person's life.

good news has real implications for people's lives. Religious conventions, cultural assumptions, class- and status-based privileges, political loyalties, and economic systems are put in peril when the missionaries come to town.

I'm convinced that many prominent aspects of twenty-first-century American Christianity are out of step with the good news Acts describes. No one in Acts blends faith with patriotism or dutiful civic devotion. Communities of faith do not become settings for individuals to seek out their own kind and avoid believers of other ethnic identities who live out their faith differently. Religious belief is no private matter in Acts; it has implications for one's spending habits, political loyalties, and social circles. A commitment to Jesus affects everything about a person's life and how a person understands his or her place in the world.

In Acts, those far-reaching implications of the good news are so apparent that even people outside of the church recognize them. Many of those outsiders conclude, with good reason, that the growing influence of the Christian message might destabilize the status quo. It will change the world even for those who reject the good news. The prospect of such changes is too much for some to handle. So they respond to the expanding ministry of the church with fear, threats, compulsion, and violence. We can learn from their reactions just how disruptive the kingdom of God can be.

Acts 14:8-20
Confusion in Lystra

As the Christian message made its way around the Mediterranean world during the first century, it didn't have to contend with religious apathy. The Greco-Roman religious landscape was vibrant and varied. People were often willing to bring their religious beliefs into creative conversation with other religious ideas. When Christian travelers brought their good news to different cultural pockets throughout the Roman Empire, the responses were not the same in each place, because different groups were operating with different religious assumptions. One way Acts gives a nod to that reality is in the fact that no two speeches in Acts are the same. The specific characteristics of each speech's audience and each set of surrounding circumstances call for making the good news understandable in a particular way. You can't translate a message without knowing something about how a target audience construes its core beliefs.

When Paul and Barnabas come to Lystra, their attempt to connect to the locals is strange and amusing. Lystra was in the south-central part of modern Turkey, about one hundred miles inland from the Mediterranean Sea. But from the perspective of certain ancient writers, Lystrans resided light years away from refined, sophisticated society. Lystra and the surrounding region of Lycaonia had a reputation as a cultural backwater. Some considered it a place that bred ignorance and superstition.

Maybe ancient readers would chuckle or nod knowingly when they got to the part in the story about the Lystrans deciding that Paul and Barnabas were gods in human form. What should you expect from those rubes? Acts is capitalizing on familiar stereotypes and poking fun at the Lystrans.

At the same time, maybe the Lystrans have good reason for their assessment of Barnabas and Paul. An ancient Roman poet named Ovid included a story about a place near Lystra in his work *Metamorphoses*. In that tale, the gods Zeus and Hermes show up disguised as human travelers. When all the residents except an elderly couple deny them hospitality, a flood destroys everyone else in the region.

Growing up near San Francisco, I was taught from an early age to recognize when an earthquake was starting and to take steps to protect myself. That's what we did there. We all had seen the photos of the destruction from the great quake of 1906. We knew enough about geology to be aware that those things happened near our home. I imagine parents and teachers in Lystra once told their children: "Remember! When travelers show up and perform deeds that ordinary people can't do, don't ignore them but treat them as deities in disguise. Otherwise we could all be toast." Part of the Lystrans' own deeply rooted cultural memory and survival instincts might have proceeded from specific foundational convictions: the gods can be capricious; they are dangerous; don't upset them.

Even when we account for that cultural background, the story in Acts 14 is still funny. There's confusion everywhere. Paul and Barnabas, who likely don't speak Lycaonian, appear unaware of what's going on around them until the priest shows up with oxen for a barbecue.

Notice Barnabas and Paul's short speech, though. It's basic. It's desperate to stop an ill-conceived sacrifice. It makes no mention of Jesus or anything so specific. It simply asserts that the one true God can be glimpsed through the natural world if we perceive it correctly. What we should focus on if we want to know God's true character isn't violence or threat or floodwaters but the rains that produce crops and sustain life. It's a sentimental sermon, and it doesn't help me understand why a loving Deity would allow earthquakes to rattle my childhood home from time to time, but it's an effort to meet the Lystrans where they are and to offer them a new religious perspective: there's only one God. Furthermore, this God isn't eager to wash anyone away in anger.

Presumably the missionaries would have gotten more specific with the audience in their second lesson, but that never happens during this visit because the Lystrans prove easily swayed and turn on Paul. One suspects they could not let go of their previous ways of making sense of the world. Those are rarely easy for anyone to surrender.

If you've ever tried to explain Christian faith to someone who has had absolutely no previous exposure to it, you know how difficult the task can be. And how absurd your explanations can sound. Where do you begin? Nothing about coming to understand the Christian message or embracing it is especially easy.

Whenever we talk about God with others, especially with people—whether they identify as Christian or not—who might be operating with very different fundamental understandings of who God is, we are rarely having just an intellectual or hypothetical discussion. We are always about an inch away from other topics that touch us where we make meaning for ourselves: how we make sense of our place in the world, what a well-lived life looks like, and what makes life truly joyful.

How do Barnabas and Paul know that God is good, is generous, and fills "hearts with joy"? They are drawing from the testimonies of many people, living and dead. What simple theological statements those are, but what potentially life-altering and liberating claims they are, too. For people to embrace them as their own theology, they may have to adjust other basic expectations they have about the world and their place in it. The good news can come across like an earthquake, shaking up the foundations of a person's worldview and rearranging everything.

Acts 16:11-40
Hostility in Philippi

Was there a legitimate place in the Roman Empire's mainstream society for Christian faith, or was God's new society destined to remain an outsider movement? Acts never puts the question quite like that, perhaps because the question as I've phrased it is too simplistic, as if it were possible to speak of only *one* kind of church or only *one* sort of mainstream society. The question is just as complex now in the modern world, and just as likely to instigate disagreements.

The events in Philippi do provoke the question, however. They make up one of the uglier and more violent chapters in Acts. It ends with all the protagonists safe and vindicated, but it's not clear that that settles the question for the long run. "Outsider status" may simply be part of the Christian church's DNA.

Philippi, a city built on a hill near gold mines and fertile farmland, was a Roman colony. That meant it maintained very close cultural and political ties to Rome—like an offshoot of Roman society transplanted way out in Macedonia. It became a colony about ninety years before the time in which the Acts story is set, because of events many English-speakers learned about when studying Shakespeare in high school. If you remember "Beware the Ides of March!" and "Et tu, Brute?" you may remember that Cassius and Brutus, two high-ranking Roman politicians, orchestrated the assassination of Julius Caesar. Those men and their forces later fell to Marc Antony and Octavian—the man who would eventually become known as "Augustus," the first Roman emperor—near the place that came to be Philippi. After that monumental battle, Octavian displaced the locals and gave land to his soldiers, rewarding them for their loyalty and courage.

About ten thousand people lived in Philippi at the time of Paul and Silas's visit—many of them either descendants of veterans who fought for the first emperor in his most momentous conflicts, or slaves and free persons with their own connections to families that could boast notable military histories.

Paul and Silas's first experience there is quiet and relatively private. They meet Lydia—a Gentile who nevertheless worships the God of Israel—outside the city near a place where she and other women go to pray. Lydia, we are told, comes from elsewhere: Thyatira, across the Aegean Sea. She's an outsider who has had to find a place beyond the city gate to practice her religion. Does she prefer to be by the river, or are there other reasons why she and others pray away from the city? Acts does not elaborate. What we do know is she becomes the charter member of Philippi's First Christian Church, and she obviously understands the worth of hospitality.

Subsequent events are much noisier. First, Paul silences a talkative spirit that empowers a slave girl with the gift of divination or fortune-telling. Those were powers many Romans associated with the deity Apollo, a very important god in Roman political propaganda. But at this point in the scene things are just comedic. A spiritual being that is known for revealing the truth simply can't stop declaring the truth about the good news: it's God's way of salvation. In doing this, the spirit is humorously announcing its own lesser significance and its own subjugation to "the Most High God." Once Paul has had enough of the acclaim, he makes the irony of the spirit's insights much less subtle. Essentially, he says, "Look what this powerful God will do to you, then." Out goes the spirit, proving its insights were accurate.

I wish Paul had invited the slave girl to join Lydia in Philippi's new Christian community. This unnamed slave now finds herself much less valuable to her owners, which will have consequences for her well-being. But she instantly leaves the stage. Paul, Silas, and the narrator treat her as expendable. Can she, too, be liberated?

Nevertheless, the scene immediately escalates in seriousness when it becomes clear that Paul and Silas have done more than angered a handful of greedy businessmen. Paul's power over the spirit strikes the Philippians as an act of aggression perpetrated by outsiders. How dare this stranger embarrass the powers of Apollo like that?

Accusations fly in the marketplace in front of magistrates, with the action now transpiring squarely in the commercial and legal center of the colony. It's not that Paul and Silas have damaged a slave (someone's property!), they are bad for Rome and therefore bad for Philippi's special standing in the Roman order. The accusers draw from common anti-Jewish tropes, painting Jews as sneaky outsiders, enemies of Roman society. Watch carefully, for we're witnessing how nationalism and xenophobia operate. The Philippians are closing ranks against anyone who threatens to pollute their narrative of their own exceptionalism.

Next come torture and incarceration—tools that desperate societies rely on when they have lost the moral courage to live up to their own honorable ideals. Later we will learn, once it becomes evident that no prison is stronger than the Holy Spirit, that the magistrates also subvert their own treasured Roman justice. They deny the privileges that Paul and Silas deserve according to Rome's own legal principles. Acts declares that the two preachers are just as Roman as anyone else in the story.

When the prison breaks open, everyone realizes that quarantining Paul and Silas is no longer an option. Then the officials responsible for making sure the colony fulfills its imperial purposes set out on different paths. First, the jailer, who had authority to shackle his inmates just a few verses earlier, abruptly finds himself trapped and desperate when the prison fails. Suddenly it's clear he's the real prisoner here, serving a system that perpetuates itself through dominance and control over others. But Paul and Silas's God has just unmasked the futility behind those displays of strength. By God's grace, though, salvation is available even for the jailer and his household. He takes it. He washes his former prisoners' wounds and feeds them. Once again, hospitality occurs.

Next, the magistrates also need a way out. They don't seek a rescue, however; they just want the problem to go away. So they dismiss Paul and Silas, even if the price of sending the outsiders off is the humiliation and fear they have to experience when the missionaries leave vindicated. Despite the magistrates' desperation to retain control, the colony's efforts to preserve some kind of cultural exceptionalism are doomed to fail. Paul and Silas didn't come to Philippi to take over the place. But they did come to transform it.

I'm a strong proponent of interfaith cooperation and understanding. My Christian convictions celebrate people of other faiths and their practices even while I live out a calling to bear humble witness to God's gracious love for the world through Jesus Christ. That's why this passage leaves me worried. A triumphalist beat can be heard, in which Paul and Silas would rather win all the religious marbles than find common cause with others. In our wonderfully pluralistic society, Paul and Silas's approach can come across as its own kind of futile attempt to grasp for dominance.

But the triumphalist beat grows softer in my ears when I realize that this passage is more concerned with making a different point, one that I also try to take seriously: there are false gods in the world, and one facet of Christian faith involves exposing how dangerous it is to serve them. That doesn't mean Christians have a duty to attack all other religions; far from it. Instead, I'm referring to the ways in which we serve the "gods" we construct with the systems and tactics our societies employ to oppress the strangers among us and to protect our traditions and privileges above anything else. At its heart, Christian faith always seeks to see people liberated from oppressive and cruel political realities.

The stories that transpire in Philippi raise the question of the church's place within the Roman world. What the stories illuminate is that the good news we announce in word and deed is a public thing—not a catalog of theological doctrines to adhere to, but a declaration that God is certainly transforming the whole world and is committed to healing our sinful selves and systems. Because of that public character, our loyalty to the good news invariably challenges moral and political structures that prefer to use dominance and humiliation to perpetuate themselves.

Acts 17:1-9

Uproar in Thessalonica

At first glance the story of Paul and Silas in Thessalonica looks like a stock scene. It contains several themes that are conspicuous in Acts: preaching in synagogues, reference to the scriptures, the necessity of Jesus' suffering and resurrection, varying responses from the same audience, some converts from high society, and strong opposition from a group of anonymous Jews (with all the problems that theme keeps bringing). Where this brief scene opens up, however, is in the description of the hostility that boils over. Some of the anger appears forced, but it confirms a couple of things that Acts has already declared to be true.

First, the accusers refer to Paul and Silas as "people who have been turning the world upside down" and who act "contrary to the decrees of the emperor, saying that there is another king named Jesus" (verses 6-7). They have a point. Those complaints recall Luke 23:1-5, when the leaders of the Temple accused Jesus before Pilate. They claimed Jesus incited the people, caused disturbances, and declared himself to be a king. Both passages include accusations that Jesus and his followers present themselves as rebellious and threatening to Roman priorities. Obviously with those calculated charges the antagonists in Thessalonica are trying to get the city authorities' attention, but no lies are being told. Paul and Silas are doing more than preaching private religion. They may not be outright political revolutionaries, but they are calling people to an allegiance to Jesus that supersedes patriotism or any other devotion to the empire.

In addition, the accusers harass a man named Jason along with other unnamed believers. Jason's crime? Hospitality. The accusations implicate him as one who harbors disruptive outsiders. There's an irony here: one of the defining characteristics of the young church in Acts has been hospitality and the fostering of community. That's a second insight the accusers have. So they use Jason's openheartedness against him. Perhaps the accusers recognize the transformative power and appeal of hospitality and so they try to prevent it from continuing. Maybe they can make the Christians wary about looking out for one another. If the accusers cannot get their hands on Silas and Paul, at least they can try to inject distrust into the community. If they can't cut off the movement's head, at least they can weaken its knees.

One of Rome's strategies for controlling its empire was to demand a loyalty that upheld the centrality of the

What if we asked, "How does your church live a common life in distinctively Christian ways? How does your congregation nourish its commitment to imitate Jesus Christ's desire to associate with so-called outsiders?" Or, "Look at how that church equips its people to work for reconciliation in its neighborhood!"

emperor and the values he represented. Fealty to Rome meant supporting a social system that was designed to ensure benefits flowed to the people who were worthy of them according to the hierarchy that held Roman culture together. The message "Jesus is Lord" on its own was not enough to imperil such loyalty. The Christian way of life, however, with its emphasis on mutuality and self-denial—that was a more serious matter.

I see ways in which this passage informs how I think about faithful living in the modern world. Speaking about the success or vitality of Christianity too often comes down to language of market share. "How many members does your congregation have?" Or, "Look at how quickly the number of 'nones' is rising!" While those are important statistics to track, they are secondary to more consequential concerns. Consider the values of the kingdom of God and what it means to manifest an alternate way of living. What if we asked, "How does your church live a common life in distinctively Christian ways? How does your congregation nourish its commitment to imitate Jesus Christ's desire to associate with so-called outsiders?" Or, "Look at how that church equips its people to work for reconciliation in its neighborhood!"

The people who manage empires and who hoard their own privileges prefer to see churches that just focus on keeping their grounds well manicured, sending a contingent to march in the July Fourth parade, and never creating space for members to turn their faith toward addressing gun violence, cruelty toward refugees, white supremacy, or wealth disparity. Tyrants and oppressors prefer the world organized as it already is. They made it that way.

Acts 19:11-41
Resistance in Ephesus

In Acts 19, Paul and his associates are dwelling in Ephesus, where they spend two years telling people about the kingdom of God and nurturing a young Christian community (Acts 19:8-10; 20:17). As Acts describes it, their public efforts attract attention from many.

Some people want in on the success. Paul serves as a conduit for God's power to deliver people from diseases and spiritual oppression, so a pack of exorcists figure they too should use the name of Jesus. To do something in someone else's "name" is to summon the power or authority associated with that person. Acts depicts the sons of Sceva as charlatans, people eager to capitalize on Paul's fame and turn a profit on the power of religion. Like others in Acts whose lust for money and influence betrays their spiritual bankruptcy, they end up disgraced and suffering.

Yet others recognize that the good news must not be a tool for monetary gain. The magic practitioners who burn their textbooks serve as positive foils to the greedy Sceva boys. They opt against selling their scrolls, even though they might be able to use the proceeds for good. This is probably because magic in the ancient world wasn't about innocently pulling rabbits from hats; many forms of popular magic attempted to manipulate spiritual powers to seize control over people to best them, embarrass them, or harm them. Better for the new Christians to make a statement about the perils of predatory spirituality and turn their backs on the huge sum of fifty thousand pieces of silver.

Both the foolish exorcists and the reformed magicians understand the economic potential of religion and its power. The latter group willingly makes financial sacrifices as part of its dedication to Jesus Christ.

I don't like the violence in the story about the opportunistic exorcists. I wish Sceva's sons were only rebuked. Yet I try to make sure my sensitivities don't prevent me from acknowledging how dangerous religious counterfeits really are. I'm referring to people who elevate themselves by using religious communities and language as their vehicle for self-promotion. Temptations to do that abound. Likewise, I think the former magicians know something about the power of religion that I often forget: its tremendous capacity either to wreck or to restore. Their decision to destroy their expensive scrolls isn't an expression of remorse or self-punishment. It's a gift to an unsuspecting world, an attempt to set people free from harm.

There are other things to note about Ephesus if we are to appreciate all the nuance of what occurs in this passage. Located on the western coast of modern Turkey, Ephesus was a prosperous and huge city, containing approximately two hundred fifty thousand residents. The fourth-largest city in the young Roman Empire, Ephesus was known for its natural resources and commercial networks. A large share of the city's reputation derived from its millennium-old associations with the Greek goddess Artemis. Devotion to the deity was a key piece of the city's religious and civic life. The magnificent temple of Artemis in Ephesus was considered one of the Seven Wonders of the ancient world. The opportunity to honor Artemis and her temple drew throngs of travelers to Ephesus. They brought money to spend.

That's why one of the local silversmiths named Demetrius gets so upset—troubled enough to start a massive demonstration that nearly swells into a riot. Demetrius keenly recognizes that the arrival and growth of Christianity in his region will be bad for business. His reasoning is simple: "Christians won't just believe differently than they used to. They'll use money differently. If they win the battle of ideas, their values will make our values look bad. Unpopular values quickly become unprofitable."

The mob is stupid (as mobs usually are). They don't even fully know "why they had come together" in the first place. But Demetrius is smart enough to appeal not only to people's pocketbooks but also to their civic pride. Artemis herself is at risk of being scorned, he says. The magnificent city will lose its identity that made it wealthy and special. Aren't the advantages that fuel Ephesian reputation and prosperity worth protecting at all costs?

The immediate crisis dissipates because a sober town clerk reminds everyone of the proper procedures and the

Roman authorities' tendency to punish rioters severely. Neither Paul nor another Christian manages to preach the good news in this scene. At the same time, someone *does* rise up and bear witness. That's Demetrius, who recognizes that the Christian faith will not allow life as usual to go unchanged in Ephesus. The old systems and privileges that he and others enjoy find themselves threatened by this new movement. It's bad news for him, because he can't or won't let go of those things. He has, as he sees it, too much to lose.

Demetrius is one of my favorite characters in Acts. He's such an appealing villain because he's deft at shaping public opinion. I like his story because he's not a member of the church but nevertheless sees clearly what the good news can do to people. He gets it. He understands the Christian movement as a force for new economic priorities and social change. From his perspective, though, some changes are too costly.

When studying this passage, I like to ask groups: what should the church's resisters be worried about in your neighborhood right now? What businesses, ideologies, or political interests have reason to feel jeopardized by the Christian witness about Jesus? And what could change if the church's members realized the influence they possess?

Christian faith, according to Acts, affects all aspects of one's life. It works to see God's desires for human existence come to fruition. Christians don't all need to support the exact same causes or take up identical positions on all political issues. But commitment to Jesus Christ is supposed to influence how we live in the world. A person's Christian faith—and eagerness to see "thy kingdom come"—should make a difference in how that person uses money, votes in elections, raises children, understands obligations to his or her neighbors, and knows when it's time to walk away from a job or some other requirement. Again, I do not believe this means there is only one "Christian way" of doing any of those things, but I do mean that we have to allow our faith to inform all aspects of our lives. Keeping our Christian faith totally isolated from our other commitments and responsibilities makes that faith no longer aligned with the kind of life Jesus lived.

Reflections

Through the centuries Christians have occasionally been guilty of mishandling Jesus' notion of "the kingdom of God" by using it as a symbol of dominance and conquest, as if we are the ones who make "the kingdom" a reality and who are supposed to rule on God's behalf. Arrogant misuses of Jesus' message have been driven by countless motives. But I see ways that these four passages from Acts can warn us about specific attitudes that can prove toxic. I have in mind how Acts occasionally describes a Christian faith that won't let itself get pushed around or that subversively relishes the opposition it encounters. In other words, there are dangers in allowing these stories to kindle an "us against them" mentality that might make us belligerent toward our neighbors. A delight in adventure, suspense, escape, and vindication winds through Acts. Don't let that style of storytelling encourage you to exchange faithfulness for nastiness.

There are also dangers in construing Christian faith in ways that seal it off from the rest of our lives. When the Holy Spirit sends the church into the empire, everyone in Acts—protagonists and antagonists alike—recognizes that there will be implications for people's social and political commitments. The Christian message and Christian living, from the most soaring public speeches to the most invisible acts of hospitality and solidarity, have the potential to change everything. That dynamic of Acts is one of the most powerful ways that the book urges its readers to dream big and expect more from their commitment to God. As I've mentioned, this makes Acts a challenging book for me and hopefully also a challenging book for congregations that have grown satisfied with merely existing and not making a difference.

Even while Acts recognizes the political implications of Christian faith, the book does not imagine that Christians will one day have the political influence they will need to make major changes in political architecture and the rise and fall of nations. How we today understand "politics" and "the state" does not map itself easily onto the political realities of 1900 years ago, when church and society were much different than they are today. None of the stories of confusion, hostility, and resistance we have explored offers clear and one-size-fits-all instructions for how Christians in any era should direct their world-changing energy.

At the same time, Acts does promote certain values that are evergreen. Those values are theological, meaning that they are rooted in our experience of God's goodness, God's commitment to deliver people from all forms of oppression, the power of reconciliation and forgiveness, and the dignity and worth of each person. Such values go beyond generic notions of "justice," "inclusion," or "trust," because they articulate specific truths we have come to learn from and about *God*. If we focus our attention on those values God has already demonstrated for us, and if we pray for God's kingdom to come, we should be equipped to live an influential faith. If we do so motivated by love and generosity, modeled on the hospitality and self-giving that reside at the heart of Christian faith, who knows where God's Spirit will guide us?

Afterword

Looking Back to Look Ahead

When walking out of a theater or finishing a book, some people prefer to have all the plotlines and complications tied up in a neat bow. I like it better when there are loose ends, when a story doesn't provide complete resolution about each detail or character. Consider me and my imagination satisfied, then, that the final words of Acts aren't: "And they all lived happily ever after."

Acts 28:30-31

The ending of a story that hasn't ended

When the curtain closes on Acts, Paul is in Rome living under house arrest while awaiting his hearing before Emperor Nero. Indications suggest it won't end well for him. Previously Paul spoke to his friends as though he expected to die soon (Acts 20:17-38). The narrative gives no reason to question his assumption that his days are numbered. Acts was written twenty-five or more years after Paul's death (which occurred between the years 60–64), and so the book's original audiences probably didn't experience any suspense about where Paul's incarceration would finally lead him. Most likely everyone knew Rome was his last stop. Other Christian writings from a later time report that Paul was indeed executed there at Nero's command, but for some reason Acts declines to tell exactly how Paul's story ended.

The reason for that is simple: Acts never set out to tell Paul's story.

If a primary purpose of the book had been to trace Paul's contributions to the existence and growth of the early church from the time Jesus called him until his death, then Acts would have a very different ending. The same is true if Acts was determined to relay everything worth knowing about the lives and deaths of the apostles.

Instead, Acts tells a story about the perseverance of the word of God. In other words, it's a book meant to convey the experiences of the early church as believers took (and continued to discover) God's good news of Jesus Christ throughout their known world. The word of God—manifested in the message about God's salvation and the Holy Spirit's transformative power—was always the story's main focus and real hero. And so God's word persists; it presses on at the end of Acts, where we read:

> He [that is, Paul] lived there two whole years at his own expense and welcomed all who came to him, proclaiming the kingdom of God and teaching about the Lord Jesus Christ with all boldness and without hindrance.
>
> (Acts 28:30–31)

Although as Rome's prisoner he's limited in his ability to circulate among the public, Paul continues to do what he's already been doing for the majority of his time on the narrative's stage: preaching and teaching. He welcomes "all,"

> The story of Acts is over, but what will happen next? Where will the unconfined word of God go? What will it stir up?

anyone in Rome who shows curiosity about him and his message, whether Jews or Gentiles. It's entirely what Jesus summoned him to do in the first place, back in Acts 9:15-16. That was when Jesus told Ananias that Paul (then known as Saul) would "bring my name before Gentiles and kings and before the people of Israel." And Paul would suffer. Now in Rome, all dimensions of Paul's ministry continue according to Jesus' original description. When Paul's life on earth is finished, others will no doubt pick up where he left off. Proclaimers of the good news come and go, but the proclamation continues.

I appreciate the irony in these verses. Paul conducts his ministry "with all boldness and without hindrance" even though he is incarcerated. The Roman Empire might control his body and restrict his movement, but no one can subdue the influence his ministry still has. The irony of Paul's circumstances directs readers to focus not on limitations but on possibilities: constraints are not as constraining as they might appear to be, and even with Paul in custody Acts continues to be a story about salvation, freedom, and renewal.

No one can take a word back after speaking it aloud; once it hits the open air, it's beyond the speaker's control. Likewise, the final word in the Greek text of Acts, *akōlutōs*, which means "unhindered," hangs in the air when the narrative ends. The story of Acts is over, but what will happen next? Where will the unconfined word of God go? What will it stir up? Where will Jesus' followers find the Holy Spirit urging them to hear the good news in fresh, expanding ways and to communicate it to others? The larger story—concerning the word of God—hasn't ended yet.

Catching up with the Spirit

As our exploration of Acts comes to a close, consider that Paul and his associates credit God with directing him through multiple perils and safely to Rome. The theme emerges in several places, both explicitly (Acts 19:21; 21:14; 23:11; 27:23-24) and implicitly.

If I'm honest, I have to confess that I don't know what it feels like to have such strong confidence in claiming *God's* unique guidance. I find it problematic to assign responsibility to God for orchestrating very specific outcomes in my life. I get wary when Christians speak that way, especially if they are doing so to express happiness when things turn out favorably for them. It's less popular to identify God as the direct cause of heartbreak, suffering, or failure.

Nevertheless, by the time we reach the end of Acts we should have learned from the narrative that the Spirit of Jesus operates in all sorts of ways. The story usually implies that there was some kind of purpose in all of the early church's history. Hindsight has its advantages. After all, one of the major objectives of the book seems to be to look back at a history full of flourishing, setbacks, dispute, and surprise and ask, "What difference does it make to assert that God was present and accompanying believers in the midst of all the great and horrible things that happened during the first decades of the church?"

We can ask a similar question: What difference does that historical memory make for Christians today? How does Acts lead us to think about God's role in our past and future? What difference does it make to say God accompanies and shepherds the church? Maybe a stubborn belief in the presence and consistency of the Holy Spirit is as good an explanation as any for a fallible church's ongoing existence.

I don't believe that Acts requires us to believe that the Holy Spirit plots a precise plan to steer Paul step-by-step to Rome. Nor must we believe that the Spirit controls every little thing in our world today. But Acts does urge us to affirm that the Spirit becomes apparent when believers bear witness together through their expressions of mutuality, solidarity, worship, reconciliation, and charity. Acts gives me confidence to say that congregations are living into the reality of the Spirit among them when they open themselves up to the fullness of God's grace, such as when they become places that are more hospitable, more inclusive, more forgiving, and more daring. Exactly why and how Paul eventually made it to Rome sometime during Nero's reign is, at the end of the day, of minimal concern to me. Believing that the Holy Spirit was present and active with him and other believers when he got there is much more useful to my ability to trust God as I navigate my life's ups and downs.

If we learn anything from Acts, let it be that the Holy Spirit has never been under the church's control, for believers in Acts learn what it means to keep in step with the Spirit by paying attention to the insights of outsiders, by wrestling with scripture together, by listening to one another's testimonies about what the good news is all about, and by boldly challenging the lies and injustices they observe in their various settings. The same Divine Spirit we read about in Acts, glimmering through memories about the experiences of ancient believers, continues even today to coax Christians toward trust and action. The Spirit, too, lives *akōlutōs*. That's what this long and occasionally wild story asks us to believe. We might catch a glimpse of the Spirit's light if we, working together, happen to find just the right angle for scrutinizing our own lives and stories—as well as the lives and stories of our neighbors.

Acts implores us: don't look back on memories about the ancient church with nostalgia. Instead, look back into Acts to reassure you about your future, for God remains as faithful as ever. Set your sights on where the word of God might be perceptible in both fresh and familiar ways now and in the days to come. We will never truly catch up with the Spirit, but we can remain in hot and joyful pursuit if we expand our outlook, committing ourselves to creative abandon and resolute hope in our shared lives. Then, what else will we discover God is making possible?

For Further Reading

These books will be useful to anyone who wants to learn more about Acts, both the content of Acts and a range of perspectives about its ongoing relevance for Christian faith and life. The ones marked with an asterisk (*) are presented in a commentary format, meaning that they walk through Acts from chapter 1 through chapter 28. As they go they comment on as many aspects of the story as space allows. The other books are either less comprehensive or organized by themes that weave their way through Acts. The list moves from books that are most accessible to readers who have little experience in exploring the Bible on their own to books that assume their readers have some familiarity with resources produced by biblical scholars.

*Hamm, Dennis. *The Acts of the Apostles.* New Collegeville Bible Commentary. Collegeville, MN: Liturgical, 2005.

This slim book belongs to a series of biblical commentaries produced by Roman Catholic scholars. In a format like an expanded study Bible, it provides basic commentary on the unfolding story and the worldviews on display in Acts. It gives information about the various geographical, historical, biblical, and cultural references that readers encounter in individual passages.

Jipp, Joshua W. *Reading Acts.* Cascade Companions. Eugene, OR: Cascade, 2018.

This short volume offers a basic introduction to Acts with chapters organized around the narrative's key theological emphases and literary structure. The book guides readers who might not know much about Acts or the early church toward discovering not only how to read Acts carefully but also how to read it as Christian scripture, with something to say about Christian belief and ministry.

Skinner, Matthew L. *Intrusive God, Disruptive Gospel: Encountering the Divine in the Book of Acts.* Grand Rapids, MI: Brazos, 2015.

I wrote this book to urge Christian readers to understand Acts as a fundamentally disruptive story, celebrating a God who upends the status quo through the spread of the good news and the creation of new communities. Short chapters examine twenty-six passages from Acts to help people appreciate and wrestle with the exciting and challenging story it tells about God, the church, and the world.

Berrigan, Daniel. *Whereon to Stand: The Acts of the Apostles and Ourselves.* Baltimore, MD: Fortkamp, 1991. Reprinted: Eugene, OR: Wipf & Stock, 2009.

Before his death in 2016, Berrigan was a Jesuit priest and vigorous public advocate for peace, disarmament, AIDS patients, and other social-justice causes. This unique book offers a series of creative meditations—some metaphorical, some rhapsodic, some theological—on each chapter in Acts, allowing Berrigan to connect the message of Acts to the passions and social consciousness that animated his faith and ministry.

*González, Justo L. *Acts: The Gospel of the Spirit.* Maryknoll, NY: Orbis Books, 2001.

This commentary was originally written in Spanish and addresses itself to Protestants living in Latin America and the United States. It investigates Acts with an eye toward the book's relevance for those audiences in the contemporary world, taking special interest in questions of justice, multiculturalism, and the character of the Christian church.

*Jennings, Willie James. *Acts.* Belief: A Theological Commentary on the Bible. Louisville, KY: Westminster John Knox, 2017.

Jennings is a specialist in Christian theology and theology's resonances among people in the African diaspora. Rich with wisdom from his expertise in those fields, this unique commentary can be described as a side-by-side and mutually informing interpretation of both Acts and modern society. A primary aim is to demonstrate that Acts depicts the church as God's means of providing people a way of connecting to one another through new communities that do not imitate the oppressive dynamics of nationalism and imperialism.

*Chance, J. Bradley. *Acts.* Smyth & Helwys Bible Commentary. Macon, GA: Smyth & Helwys, 2007.

This is a lengthy, thorough commentary but very readable even for people who have little background in the language and topics of academic biblical studies. The author pauses frequently to consider the contributions Acts makes to Christians' ways of talking about God's activity in the world and Christians' efforts to live as faithful disciples.

*Gaventa, Beverly Roberts. *Acts.* Abingdon New Testament Commentary. Nashville, TN: Abingdon, 2003.

This insightful commentary strikes a useful balance among the historical, literary, and theological dimensions of Christians' engagement with Acts. In other words, it helps readers understand the ancient historical context in which Acts is set, the value of attending to how Acts works as storytelling and history-writing, and the claims Acts makes about God, the church, and the good news.

9 781501 894558